ARTICULATE ENERGY

ARTICULATE ENERGY

ENERGY

An Inquiry into the Syntax
of English Poetry

by

DONALD DAVIE

Routledge & Kegan Paul
LONDON, HENLEY AND BOSTON

First published in 1955
Reprinted in 1965 and with a postscript in 1976
by Routledge & Kegan Paul Ltd
39, Store Street
London, WC1E 7DD
Broadway House, Newtown Road
Henley-on-Thames, Oxon RG9 1EN and
9 Park Street,
Boston, Mass. 02108, USA
Set in Monotype Fournier
and printed in Great Britain by
Redwood Burn Limited
Trowbridge & Esher
Copyright Donald Davie 1955, new material 1975

ISBN 0 7100 8155 3

CONTENTS

Page

INTRODUCTION vii

POSTSCRIPT 1975 ix

I SYNTAX AS UNPOETICAL: T. E. HULME 1

II SYNTAX AS MUSIC: SUSANNE LANGER 14

III SYNTAX AS MUSIC IN THE POETRY OF THOMAS SACKVILLE 24

IV SYNTAX AS ACTION: ERNEST FENOLLOSA 33

V SYNTAX AS ACTION IN SIDNEY, SHAKESPEARE, AND OTHERS 43

VI SYNTAX AS ACTION IN EIGHTEENTH-CENTURY POETIC THEORY 56

VII VARIETIES OF POETIC SYNTAX
1. Introduction: Grammar, and Logic 65
2. Subjective Syntax 68
3. Dramatic Syntax 76
4. Objective Syntax 79
5. Syntax like Music 85
6. Syntax like Mathematics 91

VIII SYNTAX IN ENGLISH POETRY AND IN FRENCH 96

IX SYNTAX IN THE BLANK VERSE OF WORDSWORTH'S "PRELUDE" 106

X BERKELEY AND YEATS: SYNTAX AND METRE 117

XI SYNTAX, RHETORIC, AND RHYME 130

XII THE GRAMMARIAN'S FUNERAL 142

XIII WHAT IS MODERN POETRY? 147

XIV THE REEK OF THE HUMAN 161

APPENDIX 166

INDEX 171

INTRODUCTION

THIS book is built on a very simple plan. Its earlier sections are devoted to examining three main authorities in the field of poetic theory, each of which offers, explicitly or by implication, a theory about the nature and function of syntax in poetry. Then I try to discover, simply from the reading of certain poems, the different ways in which syntax can contribute to poetic effect; and I think I show that none of the theories will quite meet the case, because the contributions of syntax are more various and often more subtle than any one of them can allow. The remainder of the book attempts to show how this discrepancy between theory and practice can obstruct our reading, and sometimes also our writing, of poetry. In case the first sections should be dry and laborious reading, I have tried here also to introduce into the exposition and criticism of theory some passages and even whole sections of a more practical kind. This has the advantage of criticizing the theories by showing how their principles work out, when adopted and applied in critical practice.

I am grateful to Douglas Brown, Professor H. O. White, and John Broadbent for helpful criticism of earlier versions of the whole work or of sections from it. And I am particularly indebted to G. Warren Shaw for permission to incorporate some of the fruits of his researches into the attitude taken up towards poetic syntax by poets and readers in the eighteenth century. Some parts of the book have appeared in rather different form in *The Twentieth Century* and in *Essays in Criticism*; and I thank the editors of these journals for permission to reprint this material.

I also thank Mr. Ezra Pound for permission to quote from

Ernest Fenollosa's essay, *The Chinese Written Character as a Medium for Poetry*; and Mr. Northrop Frye and the editor of *The Kenyon Review* for similar permission in respect of Mr. Frye's essay, *Levels of Meaning in Literature.*

POSTSCRIPT 1975

MY first book of criticism, *Purity of Diction in English Verse*, was a thinly disguised manifesto. Though this second book grew quite immediately out of that first one—from the realization that syntax was part and parcel of diction—*Articulate Energy* was or became a quite different sort of book. Whatever polemical motives I had when I started it were soon lost sight of as I recognized the excitingly un-mapped territory I had blundered into. As I began drawing the map, the work became ever more truly what I finally described it as: an Enquiry, from which whatever partialities and pre-judices I started with were gradually eliminated. Reading it over now, I still find that it has that character, genuinely an investigation by a student who has no axes to grind.

Not unnaturally, however, people who were kind enough to read the two books one after the other, and to read my poems too, supposed that there was a manifesto hidden in this book as in the earlier one. They wanted to see me as taking sides, with Pope and Yeats and perhaps Auden, against Pound and perhaps Eliot. And so these friends of mine were dis-concerted and even annoyed when a few years later I devoted a book to Pound's poetry—a book which, though it failed to please the really committed Poundians on either side of the Atlantic, on the other hand was certainly too sympathetic towards Pound, and too admiring of him, to please most British readers. And I compounded my offence later by giving respectful attention to later American poets working the Poundian vein, Charles Olson for instance, who went even further than Pound in disrupting and distorting formal syntax. Where did I stand, or where do I (for the question is still put

ix

to me)? It is not easy to answer this question without sounding self-righteous, without saying for instance that poetry, even the poetry of the last hundred years, is too wide and various a territory, and too important for the survival of our civilization, for "taking sides" to be an adequate response to it. It is a field of human study, in which bluff commonsense and evangelizing fervour are as inadequate and obstructive as they are in any other field; the coolness and impartiality which we associate with the idea of *enquiry* are as much the rules of the game in this study as in others. (Which is *not* to say that such investigations can be, or should be, "scientific"; nor is it to advocate a limp eclecticism.)

However, my friends who looked in *Articulate Energy* for a manifesto, and thought they found one, deserve a less lordly answer. The subject of the book is a limited one: syntax in poetry. Although I was surprised and a little alarmed as I worked at it, to find how many other aspects of poetry I had to touch upon, it remains true that there are whole dimensions of poetry as we have it, which had to be left out of account altogether. The histrionics of Yeats, the magnanimity of Pound —these were matters that just did not come up for discussion. And so it was entirely feasible and proper for me to prefer Yeats's handling of syntax to Pound's (as I did and do), while keeping to myself certain reservations about other aspects of these two poets' work—reservations which in a final account would tilt the balance of my sympathies the other way. My book was an investigation of poetic method, not an estimate of poetic achievements.

The older one gets, the easier it should be to maintain the impartiality of the true enquirer. But testiness too is something that comes with age. And so if I were to write the book now, it would be a testier performance, and the worse for that. As my friend Ted Weiss has written, "though with twenty years elapsed, symbolism . . . hardly dominates today", the Anglo-American poetic scene is more than ever dominated by "the intuitive, the improvisatory, the fragmentary, as against reason, syntax, order". If *Articulate Energy* reads quaintly now, it may be because of its author's ingenuous assumption that Wordsworth and Pope—Pope!—were not just standard authors reeking of the library and the examination-hall, but living presences in our poetry, challenging emulation and guiding practice. Twenty years have made a great and woeful difference here: they have seen a rapid and strident advance of the perennial and parochial fallacy that our own predicament, "the modern", is unprecedented; and accordingly the historical perspective of the poet and his readers has been drastically foreshortened. Nowadays we travel light. It sometimes seems that the most ancient author in the English language whom we acknowledge as a living presence is . . . William Blake. And even so, the Blake thus recognized as "relevant" is the author of *The Four Zoas* and *America: a Prophecy*, certainly not the master of poetic syntax whom I honour in Chapter VII. If an unprejudiced Enquiry into poetic method were undertaken nowadays, how could it be presented to an English-speaking audience which has settled all the trouble-some questions in advance, by ruling nine-tenths of the evidence inadmissible?

Some things in the book strike me now as unsatisfactory. In Chapter V the one test-case that I take from Shakespeare is not enough to vindicate Ernest Fenollosa's contentions about him, though I proceeded as if it were. Verse that is spoken by a *dramatis persona* in a fully specified dramatic situation requires, in any case, that the student take into account many more considerations than I was prepared to allow for. Then, the one comment that I permit myself on William Carlos Williams seems to me now to be wide of the mark, and in any case Williams's handling of syntax deserves more than an insolent swipe in passing. I still think that Williams's precedent and his precepts have exerted and still exert a lamentable influence, especially in the U.S.; and that no one is more responsible for what I have called the foreshortening of historical perspectives, since 1955. But another whole book would be required to substantiate this, and it is not one that I would care to write, for Williams is in many ways a very winning figure and I am affected by how much his poetry means to my American friends. It was his ambition to write an American poetry that should sever all ties with English poetry, and in this he succeeded; it is not surprising therefore that a British reader, even one like myself who has read some of his poems with pleasure, should regard his work as a whole with alarm and even a sort of rancour. I ought to have left him alone; his work has nothing to do with an enquiry into the syntax of *English* poetry. On the other hand I am quite impenitent about Dylan Thomas's sonnets, written according to principles which seem to me radically vicious. But I do something disingenuous when, in Chapter X, I slide from making this point into what looks like a discussion of Rimbaud. Thomas may have been what he called himself with bitter self-mockery, "the Rimbaud of Cwmdonkin Drive"; but this is not to say that the author of *Les Assis* and *Les Chercheuses de Poux* was the Dylan Thomas of Charleville. I can excuse myself by saying that the Welsh name and the French one were twenty years ago connected on just these lines, as by Elizabeth Sewell in a passage I discuss, and that I was considering the image of Rimbaud created by such critics, rather than Rimbaud himself. But this is not a good excuse. The least one can say is that, if indeed Thomas and Rimbaud do write themselves into the same vicious *impasse*, Rimbaud had set out from a place altogether more sane and robust and precociously splendid than any imaginative stage known to Thomas.

Some of the most careful readers of *Articulate Energy* have fastened upon those pages where I speak of a tacit compact or contract between writer and reader; and have suggested, more or less gently, that this was a graceful delusion of the mid-1950s when some of us dreamed of reconstituting a literary world like that of the eighteenth century, when author and reader alike agreed about what experiences should be brought into the public domain, what others should remain covert. (I have in mind particularly Patrick Swinden's penetrating essay, "English Poetry".[1]) I never knew any one at that time who laboured under that delusion. Instead there were certain writers who agreed with themselves to write *as if* such contracts existed between writer and reader, although they knew that they didn't exist, and couldn't. This is a quite different matter: a deliberate stratagem, undertaken so as to will into being conditions which ought to exist, but don't. And for those of us who have survived as writers from the 1950s into the 1970s it is still the only honourable stratagem that we can practise—to act *as if* the writer and his readers were still the civilized people that they may have ceased to be.

What seems to be never recognized is that some contract *must* exist between the poet and his readers, a contract which, if the poet suppresses it from his mind when he writes his poems, at least must be in his mind when he publishes them. The reader who pays hard cash for a book of poems, and then spares the time to look at what he's bought, certainly does so in the expectation of getting some return for his trouble. One remembers the perhaps legendary Frenchman in the boulevard-café who in the 1920s greeted Cocteau with "Étonne-nous, Monsieur Jean!" If the reader, when he opens a book of poems, does not look to it for the range of variously noble pleasures which the doctrine of the *genres* led him to expect, then he opens it "looking for kicks". "Étonne-nous,. Monsieur Jean . . . ", "Blow my mind, man!" A poet like Ted Hughes who in the 1950s plainly rejected the terms of the contract accepted by the Movement poets of that era, did not thereby free himself of any contractual obligations whatever. He accepted instead, as he may have learned afterwards with dismay, the terms of that grosser contract which put him on a par with Mick Jagger—as of course Allen Ginsberg did also, at about the same time. Ezra Pound, who first loosened and then rewrote the traditional contract so as to weigh it towards

[1] In *The Twentieth-Century Mind. History, Ideas, and Literature in Britain*, edited by C. B. Cox and A. E. Dyson, Volume III (1972).

the writer and against the reader, would be appalled to find that the new form of contract in effect makes the writer wholly the slave and creature of his public—a mass-public, swayed by it knows not what, capable of responding only to the grossest stimuli, at once fickle and predictable, exacting as only the undirected can be. Yet this is what has happened. And the 1960s, that hideous decade, showed what was involved: the arts of literature were enlisted on the side of all that was insane and suicidal, without order and without proportion, *against civilization*. Charles Olson in his last years was appalled by the stoned and bombed-out zombies who flocked to hear him read and lecture. *That* was not the public he thought he had been addressing! But once the poet abandons the traditional forms of contract he has no control over who shall countersign the document that is his poem.

And yet in the 1960s and today, not all poets who abandon or disrupt syntax do so for aggressive or egotistical reasons. There are some who would claim by doing so to celebrate through imitation certain natural or cosmic processes which know nothing of transitive or intransitive, of subjects, verbs, or objects:[1]

> What strikes me is how openly placed the poem is to receive whatever fruits are ripe. Mostly up to now the forms have been very tight, with theology to match and the life within purged from these two margins. And now he can hardly finish a sentence! I can't help thinking of some sweet rain falling steadily over the fields, gracefully immune to human denial; and JR moved even more than moving others, the elegist turning to psalms.

Such humility as is expressed here, such gentleness and self-effacement in poets, may be grounded in self-deception; and in any case the suppression or subversion of syntactical order may not be a necessary or logical consequence of such a sense of

[1] From advance publicity (1973) by the Grosseteste Review for John Riley's *Ways of Approaching*; a comment by J. H. Prynne on Riley's long poem, *Czargrad*.

the poet's role. But clearly, perverse or not, this is something more admirable than the strident self-aggrandisement which leads other poets to cultivate a superficially similar dishevelment—"he can hardly finish a sentence!" And indeed, I nowadays detect, under provocation from such a statement as this, another vast reach of my subject which was wholly out of my ken in 1955: how differently syntax in poetry must be regarded when poem-making is considered as a religious (celebratory) activity, rather than an ethical one. I am not much better equipped now to deal with this range of possibilities, than I was in 1955; for, as J. H. Prynne rightly hints, the question is really a theological one—whether leading the chance congregation in worship isn't the priestly function, not a poetical one.

I have changed my mind? My friends seem to think I have, not once but several times. If I have, it is nothing to be ashamed of. But it seems to me that I have not. What I wrote in 1955, I stand over now. Then what I said seemed to be timely; now it has, to my eyes, an air more forlorn. But I stand over it.

Stanford, California   Donald Davie

I

SYNTAX AS UNPOETICAL:
T. E. HULME

ᕀᕀᕀᕀᕀᕀᕀᕀᕀᕀᕀᕀᕀᕀᕀᕀᕀᕀᕀᕀᕀᕀᕀᕀᕀ

IN 1902, Hugo von Hofmannsthal, then twenty-six, published a work in prose called *The Letter of Lord Chandos*.[1]
This purports to be a letter written to Francis Bacon by an
Elizabethan nobleman, explaining why the writer has fallen
silent and dropped out of the literary life in which (as we are to
understand) he had already made his mark in his youth. It is
generally conceded that this is Hofmannsthal's rendering of a
similar crisis in his own life, a crisis which silenced him, not
completely indeed, but as a lyrical poet. For the rest of his life,
Hofmannsthal was occupied with prose and with drama, no
longer with self-sufficient poetry. *The Letter of Lord Chandos* is
not a plain allegory, and it is difficult, perhaps impossible, to
describe the crisis Hofmannsthal writes about in any other
way than as he renders it himself. Here I am interested in only
one aspect of what happens to Lord Chandos or what happened
to Hofmannsthal.

Near the beginning of the letter, Chandos speaks of his state
of mind in the days of his productive youth:

> And out of Sallust, in those happy, stimulating days, there
> flowed into me as though through never-congested conduits the

[1] Hugo von Hofmannsthal, *Selected Prose*, tr. Mary Hottinger and
Tania and James Stern, pp. 129–141.

realization of form—that deep, true, inner form which can be sensed only beyond the domain of rhetorical tricks: that form of which one can no longer say that it organizes subject-matter, for it penetrates it, dissolves it, creating at once both dream and reality, an interplay of eternal forces, something as marvellous as music or algebra. This was my most treasured plan.

This introduces at once a fancy which will recur many times in the course of this study—the notion of a literary form "as marvellous as music or algebra". This was of course an ideal of the symbolist poets, and it is not surprising that it should be in the minds of all the post-symbolist generations, up to our own day. But different writers and thinkers respond to the idea in different ways. For some it is a will o' the wisp which can lead nowhere; for some it is a baleful phantom, a night-mare; for some to whom it remains an ideal, it is all the more attractive for being unattainable, an object of wistful yearning; others believe it is attained in every successful poem. Having connected literature with music, it is natural to go on and relate it to other arts, to sculpture, painting, architecture; so Chandos compares the structure of Latin prose with the architecture of Palladio. On the other hand, if literature can be connected with mathematics, how shall it be related to science? And here again, there are many answers. Science can join hands with literature over mathematics as a bridge; or it can glare at litera-ture over mathematics as a gulf; or mathematics can be lumped with the sciences away from literature; or it can be embraced by literature and denied to the sciences; or poetry and science can fight back to back, against the mathematical abstractions that threaten both of them. This is a world, in fact, of large gestures, sweeping statements, rash conclusions, not a field for the timid or the scrupulous.

Not that this applies to Hofmannsthal. His *Letter of Lord Chandos* is a work of art, not a treatise, and if we take it as a treatise, we do so at our peril, and must take the consequences. Chandos, then, goes on to describe the state of despondency and sterility into which his buoyant arrogance has declined:

2

At first I grew by degrees incapable of discussing a loftier or more general subject in terms of which everyone, fluently and without hesitation, is wont to avail himself. I experienced an inexplicable distaste for so much as uttering the words *spirit, soul,* or *body* . . . the abstract terms of which the tongue must avail itself as a matter of course in order to voice a judgment—these terms crumbled in my mouth like mouldy fungi.

This first stage of the distemper, of which the symptom is distaste for abstract terms, comes to a head when Chandos, trying to scold his small daughter for lying, finds it impossible to distinguish, or at any rate to communicate the distinction, between truth and falsehood. This grows until the simplest propositions of common gossip seem to him "indemonstrable, as mendacious and hollow as could be". In this stage:

For me everything disintegrated into parts, those parts again into parts; no longer would anything let itself be encompassed by one idea. Single words floated round me; they congealed into eyes which stared at me and into which I was forced to stare back— whirlpools which gave me vertigo and, reeling incessantly, led into the void.

Chandos attempts to cure himself by recourse to the Ancients, not to Plato, but to Seneca and Cicero, writers notable for "the harmony of their clearly defined and orderly ideas". But in vain:

These ideas, I understood them well: I saw their wonderful interplay rise before me like magnificent fountains upon which played golden balls. I could hover around them and watch how they played, one with the other; but they were concerned only with each other, and the most profound, most personal quality of my thinking remained excluded from this magic circle.

The connection with syntax should now be clear. In his youthful buoyancy Chandos saw language as above all an instrument of articulation, a way of establishing relationships, like the harmonies of music and the equations of algebra. Syntax is one of the ways in which language is able to do this.

3

Hence, when Chandos loses his nerve (if we may put it like that), he loses, in fact, his faith in syntax. The only language he can trust is a language broken down into units of isolated words, a language which abandons any attempt at articulation, because that articulation seems to take place only inside a closed system —"they were concerned only with each other."

In *The Letter of Lord Chandos*, this change in his attitude to language is only one aspect, perhaps no more than a symptom, of a change in his attitude to experience. In his youth, he explains, he had been sure of the harmonious relationship existing between apparently quite disparate fields of experience. This I think is the point of the period-setting, for, as Hofmannsthal implies, the pastoral convention is a good example of this confidence. So too of course is the figure of Bacon himself, "the last man" (so we say in the lecture-hall) "to take the whole of human knowledge for his province", and, we may add, to take it *as* a whole. What is more, human experience was also articulated, as it were, in depth: Chandos meant to decipher the ancient fables and myths, confident (like George Chapman) of reducing them all to one articulated system; and "at other times I divined that all was allegory and that each creature was a key to all the others; and I felt myself the one capable of seizing each by the handle and unlocking as many of the others as were ready to yield." In his later phase, Chandos feels drawn to dwell upon things in themselves and in isolation. In this way, sometimes, he can attain a conviction of harmony throughout nature; but this is of a different sort. It is, specifically, un-utterable, the product of momentary sympathy with another form of life in all its uniqueness and otherness. These moments, when they come, are ecstatic, but also brief, fitful, unpredict-able. It seems that they leave behind them no residue of confidence; and the tenor of life between these revelations is distracted and inert.

Hofmannsthal, it should be realized, by creating the *persona*, Chandos, avoids committing himself on the whole issue. His detachment may even be ironical: the point may be (though I do not think it is) that the youthful confidence of Chandos was an illusion well lost; hence that syntax is a snare and a sham, and that truth is only to be found in the isolated "thing".

§ 2

Some ten or more years later, the English philosopher T. E. Hulme used the analogy of language and algebra in a quite different way:

> In prose as in algebra concrete things are embodied in signs or counters which are moved about according to rules, without being visualized at all in the process. There are in prose certain type situations and arrangements of words, which move as automatically into certain other arrangements as do functions in algebra. One only changes the Xs and the Ys back into physical things at the end of the process. Poetry, in one aspect at any rate, may be considered as an effort to avoid this characteristic of prose. It is not a counter language, but a visual concrete one. It is a compromise for a language of intuition which would hand over sensations bodily. It always endeavours to arrest you, and to make you continuously see a physical thing, to prevent you gliding through an abstract process. It chooses fresh epithets and fresh metaphors, not so much because they are new, and we are tired of the old, but because the old cease to convey a physical thing and become abstract counters. A poet says a ship "coursed the seas" to get a physical image, instead of the counter word "sailed". Visual meanings can only be transferred by the new bowl of metaphor; prose is an old pot that lets them leak out. Images in verse are not mere decoration, but the very essence of an intuitive language. Verse is a pedestrian taking you over the ground, prose—a train which delivers you at a destination.[1]

This passage, and others like it from Hulme, have had a very great influence upon English and American poets, and upon their readers, since *Speculations* was first published, in 1924. It is therefore a great pity that these writings were left by their author, fragmentary and unrevised; for Hulme's looseness in

[1] T. E. Hulme, *Speculations* (1924), pp. 134, 135.

the use of words like "abstract", "concrete", "embodied", "visualized" has survived as a persistent "woolliness" ever since and has, as we shall see, brought a needless muddle into the question of poetic syntax. If Hulme had lived to revise this material, this looseness no doubt would have been cleared away, and it should not blind us to the great power, clarity, and independence of his thought. What is more to the point here is the handful of excellent poems Hulme left behind him, which prove that when he spoke of the language of poetry he spoke with first-hand experience.

It is plain that Hulme has more in common with the later Lord Chandos than with the earlier. And it is worth noting that, like Hofmannsthal, he had abandoned writing poetry long before his death (according to Epstein, "this seemed to him too facile"), and also that, according to Sir Herbert Read, Hulme's *magnum opus* was to be "a personal philosophy, cast into an allegorical form perhaps analogous to Nietzsche's *Zarathustra*, and having as its final object the destruction of the idea that the world has unity, *or that anything can be described in words*"[1] (my italics). Yet Hulme nowhere realizes, or nowhere acknowledges, that in his view of poetic language there is no place for syntax. That this is the case should be clear to common sense, even without the parallel with Lord Chandos; but to establish the fact more firmly we need to realize what lies beneath Hulme's view of poetry, his adherence to the philosophy of Bergson. The passage I have quoted comes from the essay *Romanticism and Classicism*, but it is reproduced, almost word for word, in another called *Bergson's Theory of Art*; and it is there that it falls into place in the whole pattern of Hulme's thought.

It is probably due to Hulme that much modern criticism is Bergsonian, perhaps without knowing it. When, for instance, John Crowe Ransom writes that the poet's is a world of "stubborn and contingent objects", with a sign up, "This road does not go through to action; fictitious", he is writing quite in

[1] T. E. Hulme, *op. cit.*, p. xiv.

6

the Bergsonian spirit. Bergson distinguishes between the roads that go through to action, and those others, such as the poet's, that do not, in terms of extensive and intensive manifolds, respectively. Hulme's essay *Intensive Manifolds* is devoted to explaining these terms, but their relevance to literature is brought out in *Romanticism and Classicism*, when Hulme discusses Coleridge's use of the word "vital":

> ... Coleridge uses it in a perfectly definite and what I call dry sense. It is just this: A mechanical complexity is the sum of its parts. Put them side by side and you get the whole. Now vital or organic is merely a convenient metaphor for a complexity of a different kind, that in which the parts cannot be said to be elements as each one is modified by the other's presence, and each one to a certain extent is the whole. The leg of a chair by itself is still a leg. My leg by itself wouldn't be.
>
> Now the characteristic of the intellect is that it can only represent complexities of the mechanical kind. It can only make diagrams, and diagrams are essentially things whose parts are separate from another. The intellect always analyses—when there is a synthesis it is baffled. That is why the artist's work seems mysterious. The intellect can't represent it. This is a necessary consequence of the particular nature of the intellect and the purposes for which it is formed. It doesn't mean that your synthesis is ineffable, simply that it can't be definitely stated.
>
> Now this is all worked out in Bergson, the central feature of his whole philosophy. It is all based on the clear conception of these vital complexities which he calls "intensive", and the recognition of the fact that the intellect can only deal with the extensive multiplicity. To deal with the intensive you must use intuition.[1]

There is more about "intensive manifolds" in the essay of that name. There too we find a fuller treatment of the opposite to this, the extensive manifold:

> It is necessary then to show exactly in what way Bergson thinks that our ordinary methods of explanation distort reality. The process of explanation itself is generally quite an unconscious one. We explain things and it never strikes us to consider

[1] T. E. Hulme, *op. cit.*, pp. 138, 139.

what we have done. We are as it were *inside* the process, and we cannot observe it, but you may get a hint of its nature by observing its effects. In any explanation you start off with certain phenomena, and you transform them into something else and say: "This is what really happens." There is something about this second state that satisfies the demands of your intellect, which makes you say: "This is perfectly clear". You have in your mind a model of what is clear and comprehensible, and the process of explanation consists in expressing all the phenomena of nature in the terms of this model. I ought to say here that I am speaking not of ordinary explanation, but of explanation when it has gone to its greatest lengths, which is when it has worked itself out in any completed science like mechanics.[1]

My point is that syntax is, on this showing, an extensive manifold; and since poetry must deal with intensive manifolds, it follows that in Hulme's view poetry has no use for syntax.

We can clinch this as nearly as possible when we find Hulme making an excursion into etymology:

The question arises: Why is the intellect satisfied in this way? The answer to this is quite simple and can be got from the etymology of the words which indicate explanation. Explanation means *ex plane*, that is to say, the opening out of things on a plain surface. There is the phrase, *the chestnut explains its leaves*, i.e. unfolds them. Then the French word is *expliquer* (*explico*) to unfold. The process of explanation is always a process of unfolding. A tangled mass is unfolded flat so that you can see all its parts separated out, and any tangle which can be separated out in this way must of course be an extensive manifold.[2]

The same equation (explaining = unfolding) occurs in Ezra Pound, at one time an associate of Hulme's, when he compares Confucius with Aristotle:

Give the Greek points on explanatory elaborations. The explicitness, that is literally the unfoldedness, may be registered better in the Greek syntax, but the loss must be counted.[3]

[1] T. E. Hulme, *op. cit.*, pp. 175, 176.
[2] *Ibid.*, p. 177.
[3] *Guide to Kulchur*, p. 279.

Syntax assists explanation, but explanation is unfolding, and intensive manifolds, which should be poetry's main concern, cannot be unfolded; hence it appears that syntax is out of place in poetry.

§ 3

There is an excellent poem by Terence Tiller which expresses the view of life recommended by Hulme and Bergson, and endured, towards the end, by Hofmannsthal's Lord Chandos. (Its true paternity, I should guess, is to be found in Rilke.) And it shows too what is likely to happen to syntax, in poems that are written in this spirit. It is called "Substitutes":

> Squeezing the private sadness until words
> pearl round it, and all images become
> the private sadness and the life; and a name
> blood. Or flowering like a bride towards
> the object, amorous of image, a home:
> giving oneself to symbols; feeding myths.
>
> There is one house beyond opposing paths.
> Pelican or vampire is the same.
>
> Only by going in and not around;
> pulsing with stone's cold veins; duck's world,
>   rock's world;
> Sifting the air as trees; long as the wind;
> sucking the air as wheat; become a field.
>
> No myth will ever come to any good:
> but biting the wasp's apple; being blood.

To refuse to articulate is itself articulation; we issue the statement that we shall issue no more statements. Hence Mr. Tiller's poem closes on a full sentence. But where he wants to convey the "going in and not around", he has to dislocate the syntax of his verses.

There is poetry of the present age which goes much further than this in abnegating syntax. But it is more important to realize that syntax may have gone from a poem even when all

9

the syntactical forms in the poem are perfect and correct. If this were not the case, Hulme would have had to repudiate all the poetry written before his own day, because it is a fact that nearly all such poetry observes the forms of syntax, the forms of unfoldedness, of the extensive manifold. In fact Hulme makes no such repudiation, nor is there any need why he should. There is no harm in syntactical forms, so long as their function is perverted, so long as they are emptied of the significance they have in scientific explanation.[1] It might seem, for instance, that syntax goes out of a poem along with punctuation; but this is not the case. A poet who does without syntax may well be reluctant to write without punctuation; for (to take it on the most elementary level) the different lengths of pause signified by comma, colon, and full-stop are invaluable aids to the control of rhythm. Hence the poet may construct a complex sentence, not because the terms in the sentence are to be articulated subtly and closely, but just because he wants at that point a rhythmical unit unusually elaborate and sustained. In this case, articulation is by rhythm, and syntax only *seems* to be doing the articulating; it is a pseudo-syntax, a play of empty forms.

One way, then, to empty syntactical forms of their significance is to make them subservient to a very heavy rhythmical pattern. There are subtler ways of "emptying". Thus T. C. Pollock remarks, "Full-sentence statement is now the favoured symbolic pattern in civilized speech, especially in civilized writing, so that there exists in the minds of most educated people what we may call *an expectation of the sentence*, which results in a sense of frustration or bafflement if the words they hear or see are not arranged in conventional sentence-patterns ..."[2] Hence it would be possible for a poet to set up such

[1] This is a point missed by Mr. Howard Nemerov in an otherwise excellent brief discussion of this question with reference to the poetry of Dylan Thomas ("The Generation of Violence", *Kenyon Review*, Summer 1953, pp. 477, 478).

[2] T. C. Pollock, *The Nature of Literature*, p. 75.

frustration in his readers, only so as to reap the fuller reward when, at the end of a poem or passage, he resolves them. It would be possible to argue that Terence Tiller places a "full-sentence statement" at the end of his poem, not because what he has to say demands that form, but so as to induce in the reader a sense of well-earned composure after the frustrations caused by the incomplete syntactical forms of the earlier lines.

Again, no one maintains that syntax, as the grammarian understands the term, is the only means available to poetry for articulating experience. There is, for instance, the sort of irrational articulation that goes on in dreams. This, it could be argued, is a sort of articulation that does not involve, in Hulme's terms, an "extensive manifold". By exploiting to the full an articulation analogous to that of dreams, the poet can make the articulations of syntax, even while their forms are retained, no more than a phantasmal play on the surface of his poem. Then the true articulation takes place by magical or dream-like associations of one image with another; a word in one sentence reaches out to embrace another two sentences away, and the relationship thus established makes the relation of each word to the others in its sentence seem thin and illusory. So, once more, the forms of syntax are emptied of significance.

Of great interest, in this connection, are the admirable speculations of Elizabeth Sewell on the literature of nonsense. Hulme remarks, "As an example of the kind of thing which the intellect does consider perfectly clear and comprehensible you can think of a lot of pieces on a draught board."[1] Games like draughts or chess are perfect examples of extensive manifolds, an exercise of sheer articulation. So Elizabeth Sewell writes of Lewis Carroll,[2] "Chess and language seem to have been united in some way in Carroll's mind, as if it might be possible to manipulate words according to the principles of a game of chess, which are those of logic." Hence she finds in Carroll's writing

[1] T. E. Hulme, *op. cit.*, p. 176.
[2] "Bats and Tea-Trays: A Note on Nonsense", *Essays in Criticism*, I, 4, 376–386.

passages where the syntactical possibilities of language have been exploited so far as to usurp all others:

> If I or she should chance to be
> Involved in this affair,
> He trusts to you to set them free,
> Exactly as we were.

But this, as Miss Sewell points out, is unrepresentative because it is too easy. The point of the game is to defeat the dream on its own grounds, by using "words referring to concrete things", words which are the material of dreams, yet which shall, by skilful handling, deny to dream any foothold:

> Nonsense has to make a simple universe from material which is complex and subject, in part at least, to a force whose main activity lies in weaving networks of relations, establishing associations, identifying one element with another and both with the mind in which this process is going on, observing strange and multiple likenesses, creating the never-stable complex which is the typical product of the dreaming mind. To prevent this happening, Nonsense can do only one thing: select and organize its words in such a way as to inhibit as far as possible the dreaming mind's tendency towards the multiplication of relations. The Nonsense universe must be the sum of its parts and nothing more. There must be no fusion and synthesis, no calling in of the dream faculty to lend to the whole so formed new significances beyond the grasp of logic.

Elizabeth Sewell goes on to show in detail how Lear and Carroll go about this game. Carroll's world is as far as possible from the world of dreams. His language is the apotheosis of syntax, and there is no wonder that Miss Sewell should have moved from considering Carroll to the symbolist poet Valéry.

Now the poet who distrusts syntax has only to reverse this process. As the nonsense poet will exclude wherever possible the articulations of dream, a poet like Hulme or Tiller will build up the structure of dream in order to break down or to emasculate the logical articulations of syntax.

§ 4

I get the impression that Hulme's views about the nature of poetical language are the ideas most generally current, almost the standard ideas, among poets and their readers today, at least in the English-speaking world. We still generally assume that it is the poet's duty to exclude abstractions in favour of concretions:

> For it is part of the business of poetry to peel off the woolly overcoats of language and to break through to the bare and physical sense: the poet will seldom use an abstract word like "dynamic"; instead, he will discover a music or an image that concretely imitates a dynamic happening.[1]

As I have hinted, because Hulme originally used these terms loosely, they are frequently "woolly" today. One example is the use of "specific", often going along with "concrete" as a term of approval. Yet, as T. C. Pollock points out, "abstract and generalized linguistic forms are more useful than are concrete for making specific references."[2] Such examples could be multiplied, and may appear in due course. On the other hand, later writers have abandoned the Bergsonian element in Hulme's vocabulary, while often retaining, tacitly or unconsciously, his Bergsonian assumptions.

[1] W. R. Rodgers, "Speak and Span", *New Statesman and Nation*, Dec. 15, 1951, p. 704.
[2] T. C. Pollock, *op. cit.*, p. 75.

II

SYNTAX AS MUSIC: SUSANNE LANGER

꙳꙳꙳꙳꙳꙳꙳꙳꙳꙳꙳꙳꙳꙳꙳꙳꙳꙳꙳꙳꙳꙳꙳꙳꙳꙳꙳

WHEN Susanne Langer's *Philosophy in a New Key* was published at Harvard in 1942, it attracted little attention. Nine years later Sir Herbert Read thought this neglect comparable to the neglect of Kierkegaard's works, when they first appeared.[1] No doubt the comparison is designedly provocative; but if it is extravagant, it is not ludicrous. For *Philosophy in a New Key* is indeed a remarkable book. It ranges through many fields of speculation and knowledge, and that, I suspect, is why it was neglected; only a committee could review it properly. But one need not be an expert in any of these fields to be astonished and delighted by its grand synoptic sweep and the vigour and lucidity of its style.

I make no pretensions here to consider it as a whole. I want to examine it from only one point of view, in the light of Sir Herbert Read's claim, "For the first time we have a theory which accounts satisfactorily for all forms of art." And, to narrow the matter still further, I seek to examine this from the standpoint of only one form of art, the art of poetry.

A glance at the index advises us that if Susanne Langer has accounted for poetry, along with the other muses, she has done

[1] Sir Herbert Read, "The Language of Symbols", *World Review*, Sept. 1951, pp. 33–36.

so very succinctly. And when we turn to such comments as there are, to find in the conjuror's hat only that dowdy old rabbit, "significant form", we may well feel we can direct the author to I. A. Richards's *Principles*, and be done with it.

But this would be a mistake. Sir Herbert Read has not been gulled, and this is not just another system of aesthetics compiled by the professional philosopher, one of those books that would be so admirable if only we could be sure that the author had ever enjoyed a poem, a sonata, or a painting. Susanne Langer takes her Clive Bell with reservations; and in taking over his phrase she transforms it—chiefly because the analogy she proposes for poetry is not so much painting or ceramics, as music. As a result "significant form" comes back into the arena of serious discussion. And so does another old tag that has faded and rubbed smooth, Walter Pater's pronouncement, "All the arts aspire to the condition of music." Both these must now be taken seriously; for what in Pater was cryptic, what in Bell was vague, becomes by this handling crisp and definite.

The force of the argument, as Mrs. Langer presents it, is in her grasp of what it feels like to listen to music. This is an author who *has* enjoyed a sonata. She has enjoyed poems too, but it is the music we must start with. Because she can re-create the effect music has on the listener, we are prepared to go with her when she asks what music means, to him and to us.

What is the meaning of music? There is a passage in *The Waves* where Rhoda, having heard of the unexpected death of a friend, seeks consolation in a concert:

> Then, swollen but contained in slippery satin, the seagreen woman comes to our rescue. She sucks in her lips, assumes an air of intensity, inflates herself and hurls herself precisely at the right moment as if she saw an apple and her voice was the arrow into the note, "Ah!"
>
> An axe has split a tree to the core; the core is warm; sound quivers within the bark. "Ah!" cried a woman to her lover, leaning from her window in Venice. "Ah, ah!" she cried, and

again she cries "Ah!" She has provided us with a cry. But only a cry. And what is a cry? Then the beetle-shaped men come with their violins; wait; count; nod; down come their bows. And there is ripple and laughter like the dance of olive trees and their myriad-tongued grey leaves when a seafarer, biting a twig between his lips where the many-backed steep hills come down, leaps on shore.

"Like" and "like" and "like"—but what is the thing that lies beneath the semblance of the thing? Now that lightning has gashed the tree and the flowering branch has fallen and Percival, by his death, has made me this gift, let me see the thing. There is a square; there is an oblong. The players take the square and place it upon the oblong. They place it very accurately; they make a perfect dwelling-place. Very little is left outside. The structure is now visible; what is inchoate is here stated; we are not so various or so mean; we have made oblongs and stood them upon squares. This is our triumph; this is our consolation.[1]

This conveys admirably the paradox of musical effect, which is, on the one hand, oppressively emotional (blurted out, a cry, or a moan), on the other hand, as rigorously dry and abstract as Euclid. What is the link between these two elements?—a link, not in time, though Mrs. Woolf presents them in sequence, but in the total impression of any musical work? The link, clearly, is some sort of articulation, when the fiddles begin to weave in and out; not quite the articulation of narrative, though it may evoke narratives as fanciful similes, but more like the articulation of a painting, although it takes place in time, with first one thing then another, as a painting does not.

Such is Mrs. Langer's account of the effect of music. The crudest idea of musical meaning is that any piece of music expresses an emotion—this is a joyful piece, this one is sad; this is a cry of joy, this is a moan of pain. But the same piece may be joyful to one person, sorrowful to another. At the other extreme, the purist cries that music is shape, pattern,

[1] *The Waves* (new edition 1946), pp. 115, 116.

which means nothing but itself; but this is belied by the universal experience that music *does* stir the emotions, *is* tinged with feeling, does speak to us as to active and suffering persons. A true account of musical effect must include both these elements; and Mrs. Langer does so by saying that *"what music can actually reflect is only the morphology of feeling"*, not this feeling or that (though this one and that one swim up for an instant now here, now there), but feeling in itself, its structure. And as Mrs. Langer says, a joyful and a sorrowful feeling may have the same morphology. Its burden is, as she says, "in very naive phrase, a knowledge of 'how feelings go'." And it is there, in the "going"—in presenting how feelings are built up, how they branch and fork and coalesce—that we find the articulating back and forth that is music's life:

> Articulation is its life, but not assertion; expressiveness, not expression. The actual function of meaning, which calls for permanent contents, is not fulfilled; for the *assignment* of one rather than another possible meaning to each form is never explicitly made.

In saying this, Mrs. Langer uses "meaning" in a specially restricted sense. She certainly does not want to dismiss music as meaningless. This labour of articulation is meaning enough, she thinks, and rational meaning too; for the whole brunt of her argument is directed against thinkers like Russell, Carnap, and Wittgenstein, for whom the arts are welcome enough so long as they remain in the world of the emotive, outside the pale of reason. This is the point of her chapters on semantics, on folklore and ritual. For "the new key" of her title is the idea of symbol—this is the key that is to open new philosophical doors; and the arts, she argues, use symbols no more than language does, and no less rationally, though in a non-discursive, a "presentational" way.

This is the thorniest part of the book, though still absorbing and still beautifully lucid. For present purposes, we need only realize that for Mrs. Langer language is a discursive

17

symbolism, where music is a presentational symbolism; and that poetry, as an art, in this resembles music more than it resembles the language of speech or of prose.

This she explains as follows:

> Though the *material* of poetry is verbal, its import is not the literal assertion made in the words, but *the way the assertion is made*, and this involves the sound, the tempo, the aura of associations of the words, the long or short sequences of ideas, the wealth or poverty of transient imagery that contains them, the sudden arrest of fantasy by pure fact, or of familiar fact by sudden fantasy, the suspense of literal meaning by a sustained ambiguity resolved in a long-awaited key-word, and the unifying, all-embracing artifice of rhythm. (The tension which music achieves through dissonance, and the reorientation in each new resolution to harmony, find their equivalents in the suspensions and periodic decisions of propositional sense in poetry. Literal sense, not euphony, is the "harmonic structure" of poetry; word-melody in literature is more akin to tone-colour in music.)[1]

The first thing to say of this is that Mrs. Langer knows what it is like to read and enjoy a poem, just as she knows what it is like to hear and enjoy a sonata. Her account is true to the features of experience. As a result, she avoids the traps set for the poet who does not know music "from the inside", for the musician who does not know poetry from the inside, and for the aesthetician who too frequently knows neither.

When poets say that poetry is or ought to be like music, they often turn out to have only a naive idea of what music is. They take such musical freaks as the imitations of cuckoo-calls, or clocks, or peals of bells, as if they were central to music's nature; and so build up a theory of poetry around the equally freakish poetical device of onomatopoeia. Or else they take music to be "a cry" ("But only a cry? And what is a cry?"), and when they say that poetry is or ought to be like music, they mean by that that the only genuine poem is the lyric, and that a poem is "lyrical", other things being equal, when it dis-

[1] *Philosophy in a New Key*, pp. 260, 261.

plays a profusion of vocatives and a punctuation consisting of exclamation marks, dashes, and rows of dots. (This is the sort of thing we find, not only in late-Victorian conservatives, but in an aggressive modernist like William Carlos Williams.) Very frequently nowadays the two ideas, of poetry as cry and poetry as onomatopoeia, come together, as in *Finnegans Wake*, where the language is onomatopoeic on the one hand, on the other the metaphorical crying language of Vico's "Age of Giants". So they come together for W. R. Rodgers.[1] And Hopkins's theory of "inscape", and Rilke's doctrine, that things utter themselves through us, can be used in a similar way, to make of poetry an onomatopoeic cry. At the other extreme comes "la poésie pure", with its poems like Edith Sitwell's early pieces, that are sheer constructs of euphony, supposedly as drained of all emotive reference as (on this purist view) music is.

What distinguishes Mrs. Langer's from all these other accounts of the poetry-music relationship is her insistence on music as pre-eminently articulation. In her view a poem is like a piece of music in that it articulates itself; and in thus establishing internal relations, establishes also relations of feeling, building up the structure, the morphology of feeling, and telling us "what it feels like to feel". In other words, the central act, of poetry as of music, is the creation of syntax, of meaningful arrangement. And hence (this seems to me the most salutary implication) the unit of poetry is not the "passage", but *the poem*.

And yet the syntax we speak of here is not the syntax of prose, that is a part of formal grammar. There is no need for the poet to preserve even *the forms* of prose-syntax; and as a result we must not suppose, whenever we find a poet who dislocates prose-syntax, that we have to deal with the poetry of the blurted-out ejaculation, the cry. The dislocated syntax of Ezra Pound in the *Cantos* may look like the dislocated syntax of William Carlos Williams, but in fact of course the *Cantos* are,

[1] W. R. Rodgers, "Speak and Span", *The New Statesman and Nation*, Dec. 15, 1951.

or are meant to be, articulated most closely. They are articulated, however, by a syntax that is musical, not linguistic, by "the unifying, all-embracing artifice of rhythm", understood in its widest sense, to mean not only the rhythm that rides through tempo and metre in the verse-paragraph, but also the rhythmical recurrence of ideas hinted at in one canto, picked up in another much later, suspended for many more, and so on.[1] The *Cantos* indeed fit Mrs. Langer's account very well.

But there are poets whose poetry "aspires to the condition of music", who nevertheless preserve the forms of linguistic syntax, as Pound does not. And it is these poets who are provided for in Mrs. Langer's parenthesis. It is their poetry, not Pound's, of which one may say that "the tension which music achieves through dissonance, and the reorientation in each new resolution to harmony, find their equivalents in the suspensions and periodic decisions of propositional sense in poetry." Perhaps the clearest example of a poet of this sort is Valéry; I happened to read Elizabeth Sewell's *Valéry* at about the same time as Mrs. Langer's book, and the poet's view of poetry chimed in so well with the philosopher's that one would think the latter had written with this poet, of all others, in mind. Valéry saw very clearly that music is not a cry, but above all an articulation:

> The pythoness could not dictate a poem. Only a line—that is to say a unit—and then another. This goddess of the continuum is incapable of continuity.[2]

And *La Jeune Parque* was first envisaged as "an operatic recitative, à la Gluck: 30 or 40 lines in one long phrase almost; and for contralto voice."[3]

But it is time to unravel the implications of Mrs. Langer's

[1] See Hugh Kenner, *The Poetry of Ezra Pound*, pp. 112–115, 274–285.

[2] Quoted by Elizabeth Sewell, *Paul Valéry: the Mind in the Mirror*, p. 28.

[3] Quoted in *Times Literary Supplement*, Aug. 22, 1952, review of *Lettres à Quelques-Uns*.

persuasive formulation. And they are clear enough. In her view, the poet suspends the propositional sense through a long verse-period, not because the sense has to be qualified before it can be completed, but so as to achieve "the tension which music achieves through dissonance"; and he decides the sense, bringing the period to a close, not because he is now prepared to commit himself to an assertion, but just to find an equivalent for music's "reorientation in each new resolution to harmony". The whole play of literal meaning, in fact, is a Swedish drill, in which nothing is being lifted, transported, or set down, though the muscles tense, knot, and relax as if it were. This is what Mrs. Langer means by saying that "Literal sense . . . is the 'harmonic structure' of poetry."

Milton can be taken on Mrs. Langer's terms:

> It is only in the period that the wave-length of Milton's verse is to be found: it is his ability to give a perfect and unique pattern to every paragraph, such that the full beauty of the line is found in its context, and his ability to work in larger musical units than any other poet—that is to me the most conclusive evidence of Milton's supreme mastery. The peculiar feeling, almost a physical sensation of a breathless leap, communicated by Milton's long periods, and by his alone, is impossible to procure from rhymed verse.[1]

So long as Milton does not "justify God's ways to man", but only, quite precisely, "goes through the motions", we can read him as if he were Valéry, and Mr. Eliot can admire him.

It is plain that Mrs. Langer's sort of poetry, where it retains forms of prosaic syntax, only seems to make use of them. And to that extent the things it says are still, in the time-honoured phrase, pseudo-statements. Mrs. Langer insists that they are not "pseudo-" in the way that I. A. Richards supposed; they are not irrational and crudely emotive like a strangled cry, the hoot of an owl, or the howl of a wolf. The statements of poetry, in her account, are like the statements of music, rational and

---

[1] T. S. Eliot, *Milton*, the British Academy Lecture.

meaningful as the hub or nest of articulations. But to the common reader the statements of poetry, even on this showing, are still "pseudo", though in a different way. They are pseudo-statements in that they do not mean what they say; the poet will not stand by them, nor take his stand upon them. "The actual function of meaning, which calls for permanent contents, is not fulfilled; for the *assignment* of one rather than another possible meaning to each form is never explicitly made."

Mrs. Langer's position on this matter is made very plain in a passage from her more recent book, *Feeling and Form:*

> ... all poetry is a creation of illusory events, even when it looks like a statement of opinions philosophical or political or aesthetic. The occurrence of a thought is an event in a thinker's personal history, and has as distinct a qualitative character as an adventure, a sight, or a human contact; it is not a proposition, but the entertainment of one, which necessarily involves vital tensions, feelings, the imminence of other thoughts, and the echoes of past thinking. Poetic reflections, therefore, are not essentially trains of logical reasoning, though they may incorporate fragments, at least, of discursive argument. Essentially they create the *semblance* of reasoning; of the seriousness, strain and progress, the sense of growing knowledge, growing clearness, conviction, and acceptance—the whole experience of philosophical thinking.
>
> Of course a poet usually builds a philosophical poem around an idea that strikes him, at the time, as true and important; but not for the sake of debating it. He accepts it and exhibits its emotional value and imaginative possibilities. Consider the Platonic doctrine of transcendental remembrance in Wordsworth's "Ode: Intimations of Immortality" ...[1]

Here Mrs. Langer, the disciple of Cassirer, stands shoulder to shoulder with T. E. Hulme and the other disciples of Bergson. Miss Rosemund Tuve has pointed out that, for the latter, poetry has to do with "a man having thoughts", not with "the thoughts a man had"; and on this showing Mrs. Langer agrees

[1] *Feeling and Form*, p. 219.

with them. For her, too, when a poet seems to speak about the thoughts he has had, he is really speaking about himself in the process of having them. And so, when the poet uses the syntactical form of the logical proposition, this form is empty, phantasmal, a sleight of hand. Thus Susanne Langer and T. E. Hulme by very different routes reach the same conclusion: that the syntactical forms used in poetry may or may not be identical with those of prose; but that, where they are identical, this identity of form masks an entirely different function.

III

SYNTAX AS MUSIC IN THE POETRY
OF THOMAS SACKVILLE

෴෴෴෴෴෴෴෴෴෴෴෴෴෴෴෴෴෴෴෴෴෴

I F we reject Mrs. Langer's analysis as a full account of the
nature of poetic syntax, we have still to acknowledge that
to take the play of syntax on her terms can illuminate certain
poetic effects which previously could not be rationalized. It is
worth taking a case which shows the advantages, if also the
limitations, of examining poetic syntax from her point of view.
This will be all the more effective if we find a case quite remote
in time and kind from symbolist and post-symbolist verse. I
propose to examine from this point of view two poems by
Thomas Sackville from the sixteenth-century *Mirror for Magi-
strates.*

Sackville in one of the best passages of the "Complaint of
Henrie Duke of Buckinghame" (which seems to me, incidentally, quite as good as the better known "Induction") rings the
changes, through several stanzas, on one simple but effective
syntactical arrangement. In stanzas 142, 143, Buckingham is
made to apostrophize Rome and reproach her for her ungrate-
ful treatment of the patriot Camillus:

> Rome thou that once advaunced up so hie
> thie staie, patron, and flour of excelence
> hast now throwen him to depth of miserie
> exiled him that was thie hole defence

> ne comptes it not a horrible offence
> to reaven him of honnour and of fame
> that wan yt the whan thou had lost the same.

> Behold Camillus he that erst revived
> the state of Rome that dienge he did find
> of his own state is now alas deprived
> banisht by them whom he did thus detbind
> that cruell age unthankfull and unkind
> declared well their fals unconstancie
> and fortune eke her mutabilitie.

The construction "exiled him that was thie hole defence" is natural enough and would go unnoticed were it not echoed almost at once:

> to reaven him of honnour and of fame
> that wan yt the whan thou had lost the same,

and echoed again in the next stanza:

> banisht by them whom he did thus detbind.

The little tune comes again and again, restated in each of the next three stanzas. Buckingham apostrophizes Scipio, who

> art now exild as though thow not deserved
> to rest in her whom thow had so preserved.

He turns again on Rome:

> Ingratefull Rome hast shewed thie crueltie
> On him by whom thow livest yet in fame.

And finally, approving Scipio's contemptuous gesture,

> his cinders yet lo doth he them denie
> that him denied amongst them for to die.

The sentence itself has a little tragic plot, with the peripeteia at the turn on the relative pronoun. As Miss Rosemond Tuve has said so well, to handle syntax with this nicety is to come as near as may be to the impossible ideal of a silent eloquence.

And this is a way of handling syntax for which neither Hulme nor Mrs. Langer makes provision.

On the other hand, there is, in the "Complaint", a justly famous lyrical digression on sleep and night (stanzas 159, 160, 161). While the beauty and pathos of these stanzas is acknowledged, I do not know that anyone has tried to account for their powerful effect, coming where they do. To do so, one needs to quote not the three stanzas alone, but a block of seven; and then to have recourse to Mrs. Langer:

> For by this wretch I being strait bewraied
> to one John mitton shreif of shropshere then
> all sodenlie was taken and convaied
> to Salsburie with rout of harnest men
> unto King Richard ther encamped then
> fast by the citie with a mightie host
> withouten dome wher hed and lief I lost.

> And with those wordes as if the ax even there
> dismembred had his hed and corps apart
> ded fell he doune and we in wofull feare
> amasd beheld him when he wold revart
> but griefes on griefes stil heapt about his hart
> that still he laie somtime revivd with pain
> and with a sigh becoming ded againe.

> Mid night was come and everie vitall thing
> with swete sound slepe their wearie lims did rest
> the bestes were still the litle burdes that sing
> now sweteli slept beside their mothers brest
> the old and all were shrouded in their nest
> the waters calm the cruell seas did cesse
> the woods and feldes and all things held their peace

> The golden stars weare whirld amid their race
> and on the erth did laugh with twinkling light
> when ech thing nestled in his resting place
> forgat daies pain withe plesure of the night
> the hare had not the gredy houndes in sight
> the ferfull dere of deth stode not in doubt
> the partridge dremd not of the sparhaukes fote

26

The ouglie bear now minded not the stake
nor how the cruel mastives did him tere
the stag laie stil unroused from the brake
the fomie bore ferd not the hunters spere
al thing was stil in desert bush and brere
with quiet hart now from their travels cest
soundlie they slept in midst of all their rest.

Whan Buckingham amid his plaint opprest
with surging sorowes and with pinching paines
in sorte thus sowned and with a sigh he cest
to tellen furth the trecherie and the traines
of Banaster which him so sore distraines
that from a sigh he fals in to a sound
and from a sound lieth raging on the ground

So twitching wear the panges that he assaied
and he so sore with rufull rage distraught
To think upon the wretche that him betraied
whome erst he made a gentleman of nought
That more and more agreved with this thought
he stormes out sights and with redoubled sore
Shryke with the furies rageth more and more.

It is plain that if a modern editor were to punctuate this, he would make one sentence of stanza 157 (the first quoted) and probably of 158 also. Stanza 159 however contains six sentences, 160 has four, 161 has five, 162 and 163, resuming the narrative, seem to make up one sentence between them. In fact, it seems to be Sackville's normal procedure to make the metrical unit (the stanza) the grammatical unit also. From this flowing melody, it is easy for Sackville to modulate into a plangent strain by putting into the stanza several short and simple, poignant sentences. (Of course this does not "explain" the effect; not all the eloquence is silent, and we certainly need Dr. Swart's[1] admirable account of Sackville's diction.)

[1] J. Swart, *Thomas Sackville: A Study in Sixteenth-Century Poetry*, Groningen Studies in English, I (Groningen, 1949).

It is plain that we have, in Sackville's lyrical digression on sleep, a clear example of the sort of poetic syntax that Susanne Langer led us to envisage. We admitted as much by the musical analogy we had to use—"From this flowing melody, it is easy ... to modulate into a plangent·strain." This, of course, is something that could have occurred to any critic, whether he had read Susanne Langer or not. (In fact, I had noted it in just those terms before reading *Philosophy in a New Key*.) But this is true, I suggest, only because Sackville is working on a large scale and the machinery of his effects is correspondingly massive. The example is an obvious one; but it seems clear that effects no different in kind can be detected, once we are prepared for them, within the compass of a sonnet. And this is the value of Mrs. Langer's note about musical equivalents for "the suspensions and periodic decisions of propositional sense in poetry".

What Sackville has to say in the stanzas about night does not exact from him the peculiar syntactical arrangements he finds for it. On the contrary the first two of the stanzas we quoted, being simple narrative, seem to demand a syntax much simpler than the complex sentences Sackville finds for them:

> For by this wretch I being strait bewraied
> to one John mitton shreif of shropshere then
> all sodenlie was taken and convaied
> to Salsburie with rout of harnest men
> unto King Richard ther encamped then
> fast by the citie with a mightie host
> withouten dome wher hed and lief I lost.

There is no articulation of meaning (e.g. of cause and effect) to compel each clause to grow out of the one before it, as each one does. Of course the syntax and the sense are not at odds, as they would have been, for instance, if we were here learning for the first time of Buckingham's death by execution. (If that had been the case, then to put the momentous information in a last subordinate clause would give it a ludicrous air, as of a careless afterthought—there is a passage in Wordsworth's "Vaudra-cour and Julia" where this happens.) Still the sense does not demand a particular syntactical form, in the way that Camillus and Scipio demand the syntax Sackville gives them. The arc of their career in public life is the arc described by the sentences which describe it—"banisht by them whom he did thus detbind." Here the turn on the pronoun is not a matter of convenience but of necessity, if the curve of syntax is to reproduce the curve of destiny.

The distinction is not a fine one, though here it may seem to be niggling. Camillus and Scipio ride through on a syntax which is the authentic thing, which does what it appears to do. The syntax of the stanzas on night and sleep appears to be collecting *exempla*; in fact, it is the servant of a plangent rhythm, stopping and starting as the rhythm commands.

Of course I have used a musical metaphor for the Camillus-Scipio passage also. The recurrent syntactical arrangement is "a little tune". But this is natural. Just as Sackville takes care in the "Induction" not to let his syntax come to blows with his sense, so here in the "Complaint" he takes care to profit by his fidelity to the sense, to make music on a recurrent motif. No doubt in the greatest poetry sense and music go together so closely that it is impossible to say that one came before the other. Nevertheless the distinction remains, and I insist it is a crucial one.

This use of "music"—"the music of the poem"—is far from satisfactory. To speak of "sense and music" in a poem is not a great deal better than saying "sense and sound", a phrase time-honoured in other connections but quite out of place here. The trouble is that music can be heard, and so when we speak of the music of verse, we think at once of those elements in poetry, phonetic and rhythmical, that likewise appeal to the ear. But when we speak of music in relation to poetic syntax, we mean something that can be appreciated in silent reading without the reader having to imagine how the poem would sound if it were uttered aloud. This is a silent music, a matter of tensions and resolutions, of movements (but again not rhythmical movements) sustained or broken, of ease or effort, rapidity or languor. What we mean, in fact, is *empathy*. Empathy occurs in our response to the plastic arts when "we feel ourselves occupying with our senses the *Gestalt* of the rising column or the spatial design of a picture."[1] Sir Herbert Read warns us regarding empathy, that "in general our use of the word in literary criticism can only be analogical." Yet he agrees that "there may be a true empathic relationship to the sound and shape of a poem—our response to metre, for example." It is Susanne Langer's achievement to have shown that our response to syntax can be "a true empathic relationship" also.

Perhaps this appears most clearly in respect of pace. We are accustomed to think, quite rightly too, that trisyllabic metre is more rapid than the iambic:

> The Assyrian came down like the wolf on the fold,
> And his cohorts were gleaming in purple and gold.

We certainly get the impression, which may even be true to fact, that in reading these lines (even silently) we have read twenty-four syllables in the time we take, in iambic verse, for sixteen. Hence we call it rapid. But now consider Pope:

> The thriving plants ignoble broomsticks made,
> Now sweep those Alleys they were born to shade

Here too, in this iambic verse, we get an impression of rapidity, but of a quite different sort. This is rapid because it expresses so much in so short a time. The rapidity of Byron is a rapid movement of lips and tongue; Pope's rapidity is a rapid movement of the mind. Pope's rapidity we perceive by empathy; Byron's we do not.

T. S. Eliot has remarked, "I know ... that a poem or a section of a poem tends to appear first in the shape of a rhythm before developing into words, and that this rhythm is capable

---

[1] Sir Herbert Read, "The Critic as Man of Feeling", *Kenyon Review*, XII, 4 (Autumn 1950), p. 577.

of giving birth to the idea and the image." And Schiller says, "When I sit down to write a poem, what I most frequently see before me is its musical element and not a clear 'idea of the subject, about which I am often not entirely clear myself." Both these statements are cited by Daniel-Henry Kahnweiler, in his book on Juan Gris,[1] at a point where he is arguing that Gris, too, got the first idea for a canvas in terms of a spatial rhythm. This rhythm, worked out in preliminary drawing and then transferred to the canvas, produced shapes which were only at a relatively late stage in the composition "modified" (to use Gris' own term) into the semblance of a guitar, a bowl of fruit, a coffee-mill, or whatever else.

If Kahnweiler is right, certainly Gris' procedure is precisely analogous to what both Schiller and Eliot record as their own ways of going to work. Yet "rhythm" and "musical element" are not necessarily the same thing. Whatever Schiller meant by "musical element", we cannot help but relate it to what has just been established as the soundless music of poetic syntax.

Interesting in this connection is a passage some pages earlier in Kahnweiler's book (pp. 100, 101), where he considers Thierry-Maulnier's remark on rhythm in poetry, to the effect that "it only exists where the repeated and regular shocks of an exact mechanism maintain the soul in a sort of vigilant torpor like the mysterious receptivity of a medium, so that everything is excluded which is not the pure suspense in anticipation of the unforeseeable." The trouble with this is the emphasis on regularity, which seems to reduce rhythm to metre. Ignore this (as Kahnweiler for his quite different purposes has to do), and the "exact mechanism", producing "the pure suspense in anticipation of the unforeseeable", could be taken to describe a piece of complex poetic syntax no less than a piece of complex and sounding rhythm. Indeed such syntax *is* rhythm, but soundless. And after all the rhythm in the head of the poet before he starts to write is soundless, in any case. We need Thierry-Maulnier's expressions to define the effect of such elaborate

[1] *Juan Gris: His Life and Work*, tr. Douglas Cooper (1947), p. 104.

poetic syntax as that of F. T. Prince in his "Epistle to a patron."[1] The sounded rhythm of that poem is very loose indeed. It can afford to be, but only because the unsounded rhythm of the syntax is so elaborately strict.

Thus, if all poems are born as rhythms, then some, it seems, may be born as rhythms of ideas, that is, as patterns of syntax rather than patterns of sound. And this would make of syntax the very nerve of poetry.

[1] See *post*, p. 92.

IV

SYNTAX AS ACTION: ERNEST FENOLLOSA

~~~~~~

I HAVE spoken, in discussing Sackville, of a sentence as having a tragic plot. This idea I owe to a cryptic comment by Mr. H. M. McLuhan on some lines of Pope, and to some illuminating pages in Hugh Kenner's *Poetry of Ezra Pound*. With the latter as my clue (I am much indebted to Mr. Kenner), I traced this notion back to Ernest Fenollosa's essay on "The Chinese Written Character as a Medium for Poetry". And this is the next document I want to consider.[1]

In the period when Ezra Pound was "spotting the winners" with such astonishing consistency, he came across the work of the orientalist Ernest Fenollosa, and subsequently prepared for publication this essay discovered among Fenollosa's papers after his death in 1908. It has never had the recognition it deserves. For Pound's flair had not deserted him. He subtitles the essay, "An Ars Poetica", and the claim is no presumptuous one. In its massive conciseness, Fenollosa's little treatise is perhaps the only English document of our time fit to rank with Sidney's *Apologie*, and the Preface to *Lyrical Ballads*, and Shelley's *Defence*, the great poetic manifestos of the past.

[1] All quotations are from the edition by John Kasper, New York, in the Square Dollar series, where Fenollosa's essay appears along with two translations from Confucius by Ezra Pound.

33

This is a matter of intrinsic value, not historical importance. For while the essay has already been influential (chiefly through the agency of Pound), it has not yet exerted the influence it deserves. We know as we read, in default of any historical evidence, that this is a great seminal work, speaking with the authority of a devoted and passionate solitary thinker.

Syntax, we have argued, is a silent eloquence, not in any hyperbolical sense, but quite literally. For syntax, we have shown, can be rapid, for instance, in a way that has nothing to do with rapid movements of lips and tongue as we read, or imagine ourselves reading, aloud. If we approach Fenollosa from this point, the relevance of his essay is apparent from the start. For the problem with which he begins is as follows: Is there anything in common between "The curfew tolls the knell of parting day", and the Chinese line, consisting of five characters the sound of which is unknown, "Moon Rays Like Pure Snow"? If there is something in common between them, then this (so Fenollosa audaciously suggests) may be taken as the essential element in poetic form.

He answers his own question by saying that what they have in common is a sort of significant sequaciousness, "the transference of force from agent to object". For "we do not always sufficiently consider that thought is successive, not through some accident or weakness of our subjective operations but because the operations of nature are successive." And "one superiority of verbal poetry as an *art* rests in its getting back to the fundamental reality of *time*." Fenollosa points out that music does this, but painting does not.

According to Fenollosa, the uniquely poetical value of Chinese rests in its combining this temporal (sequacious) feature with the density and angularity of "things", the peculiar contribution of painting and sculpture. It is thus, as it were, both music and painting. In the Chinese sentence "Man Sees Horse", we perceive that

Chinese notation is something much more than arbitrary symbols. It is based upon a vivid shorthand picture of the operations of nature. In the algebraic figure and in the spoken word there is no natural connection between thing and sign: all depends upon sheer convention. But the Chinese method follows natural suggestion. First stands the man on his two legs. Second, his eye moves through space: a bold figure represented by running legs under an eye, a modified picture of an eye, a modified picture of running legs, but unforgettable once you have seen it. Third stands the horse on his four legs.

Fenollosa, of course, reproduces the Chinese characters in question, and from them one sees clearly that the characters are as he says stylized pictures from nature, yet set in motion, moving pictures, musical and graphic at once.

Fenollosa goes on to show that this obtains inside the single character, no less than in the syntactical arrangements of several characters together:

A true noun, an isolated thing, does not exist in nature. Things are only the terminal points, or rather the meeting points, of actions, cross-sections cut through actions, snapshots. Neither can a pure verb, an abstract motion, be possible in nature. The eye sees noun and verb as one: things in motion, motion in things, and so the Chinese conception tends to represent them.

The sun underlying the bursting forth of plants =spring.
The sun sign tangled in the branches of the tree sign =east.
"Rice-field" plus "struggle" =male.
"Boat" plus "water" =boat-water, a ripple.

Pound gives, as an example of this noun-verb in English, "dog *attending* man =dogs him".

What is the moral of this for poetry in English? Fenollosa argues that English is like Chinese in lacking inflections, and that English poets can therefore learn from Chinese usage.

As regards syntax, the moral that Fenollosa draws from Chinese usage is this: the uniquely poetic, because uniquely truthful, syntactical form is the transitive sentence:

The sentence form was forced upon primitive men by nature itself. It was not we who made it; it was a reflection of the temporal order in causation. All truth has to be expressed in sentences because all truth is the *transference of power*. The type of sentence in nature is a flash of lightning. It passes between two terms, a cloud and the earth. No unit of natural process can be less than this. All natural processes are, in their units, as much as this. Light, heat, gravity, chemical affinity, human will, have this in common, that they redistribute force. Their unit of process can be represented as:

term		transference		term
from	→	of	→	to
which		force		which

If we regard this transference as the conscious or unconscious act of an agent we can translate the diagram into:

agent → act → object

In this the act is the very substance of the fact denoted. The agent and the object are only limiting terms.

It seems to me that the normal and typical sentence in English as well as in Chinese expresses just this unit of natural process. It consists of three necessary words: the first denoting the agent or subject from which the act starts, the second embodying the very stroke of the act, the third pointing to the object, the receiver of the impact. Thus:

Farmer pounds rice

the form of the Chinese transitive sentence, and of the English (omitting particles), exactly corresponds to this universal form of action in nature. This brings language close to *things*, and in its strong reliance upon verbs it erects all speech into a kind of dramatic poetry.

According to Fenollosa, the "unpoetical" intransitive verbs in English should in poetry be made transitive, wherever possible. Even negations in his view are really active, because in nature force is required to annihilate, and a negation can therefore, and should, be expressed poetically by a transitive verb. Finally the mere copula "is" should be avoided, and transitive verbs substituted:

There is in reality no such verb as a pure copula, no such original conception; our very word *exist* means "to stand forth", to show oneself by a definite act. "Is" comes from the Aryan root *as*, to breathe. "Be" is from *bhu*, to grow.

As regards the choice of single words other than verbs, Fenollosa draws from Chinese the rule that such other parts of speech should always manifest their origin in verbs, as it seems Chinese words do. Pound gives one of the relatively rare examples of such a verbal family in English: the verb, to shine; the adjective, shining; the noun, shine or sheen. So in Chinese a seeming noun, "farmer", is a verb, "one who farms". A seeming adjective, "bright" = "which shines". Prepositions: "off" = what is thrown away from; "by" = what is used to effect something; "to" = what falls towards. Conjunctions: "and" = to be included under one; "or" = to partake; "if" = to permit. Even pronouns are the same: thus Chinese has five forms of "I", differing according to the sort of thing "I" is set to do.

So far, says Fenollosa, for poetry of the seen; what of the poetry of the unseen, which deals with "lofty thoughts, spiritual suggestions, and obscure relations"? He deals with this in the way we might expect, appealing to etymology to show that the abstract words used for these topics have their root "in direct action". It is the poet's duty to reveal these concretions at the base of any abstract word, even as he uses it. This is one of the less original parts of the essay, though expressed with great force and beauty. Fenollosa points out that it is easy, in a phonetic language like English, to overlook the metaphorical roots of the abstract word, and hence to blur "the ancient lines of advance". It is much harder for a Chinese to miss them, painted into the character.

§ 2

It will be apparent that in his dislike of a language of "arbitrary symbols" such as algebra, in his pleasure when language comes "close to *things*", in his use of etymology to establish concretions under abstractions, Fenollosa is ranged with T. E Hulme rather than Susanne Langer. But he goes far beyond Hulme in that he finds room in his theory for a syntax that is not mere formalism. It is true that he has room for only one syntactical form, a very simple one; but most people would agree that this syntactical form is the basis of all the rest; and, such as it is, it is absolutely central to Fenollosa's conception of poetic language. It was the great disadvantage of Hulme's system that it found no room for syntax at all; from his point of view poetry could only grow more and more inarticulate until at last it fell silent altogether. Fenollosa, as insistent as Hulme that poetry should get close to "things", realized as Hulme did not that "things" were bundles of energies, always on the move, transmitting or receiving currents of force. Hence syntax was necessary to poetry.

Hulme and Fenollosa differ more profoundly. Fenollosa is a humanist. His appeal is always to "nature". He will accept no vindication of syntax short of that which makes it the Aristotelean imitation of a natural process. Moreover he appeals to nature in a pre-Wordsworthian way. His "nature" is the nature of John Locke. This is the clue to his audacity, which is often breathtaking. He makes the astounding claim to establish a norm, a single authentic pattern, for all human thought—the pattern of the transitive sentence. He takes for granted what Hulme, holding fast to original sin, could never admit, that "there is no disharmony between man and the outside world", that "they are both on the same level, on which man feels himself one with nature and not separate from it."[1] It would, for instance, be possible to attack Fenollosa's system at the root, by objecting that as man is an immortal spirit, it is no way to the perfection of language or of any other human institution to make it conform to the patterns of fallen nature. It seems that Fenollosa never conceived of such an objection. His humanist convictions, rare in his own day and rarer still in ours, give to

[1] T. E. Hulme.

his thought a clarity and an assurance that is positively Augustan. This eighteenth-century air is no accident, as we shall see.

Hulme in effect excludes syntax from poetry altogether. Fenollosa admits it, and values it highly, but only so long as it preserves a primitive austerity. He finds no more room than Hulme does for an elaborate verbal syntax analogous to the mathematical syntax of modern physics. Things, Fenollosa had said, are only "the terminal points ... of actions", but in the act he corrected himself—"or rather meeting-points". The correction gives the show away. If the action goes on after the end of the sentence, if it was already approaching before the sentence began, then to begin the sentence with an agent, to end it with an object, is a quite arbitrary carving out of an artificial unit from what is a continuous flow. And the argument, from the imitation of a natural process, falls to the ground.

§ 3

It may be naive of me to read Fenollosa *au pied de la lettre*, but he seems to be sufficiently categorical. He delivers a number of precepts: that the good poet will use, wherever possible, the full sentence driving through a transitive verb; that he will avoid, wherever possible, the copula; that he will rearrange, wherever possible, negations, so as to use a positive verb of negation; that he will avoid intransitive verbs; that he will be fond of verbs and cut down as far as possible the use of other parts of speech;[1] that when he uses an abstract word he will draw attention, by his use of it, to its etymological growth out of concrete actions; that in using parts of speech other than verbs he will choose wherever possible words that reveal in themselves verbal elements or origins. That is enough to be going on with; and I now propose to see what happens to our

[1] Cf. Gumilev, "Thought is movement, and poets should use verbs and not adjectives," quoted by Marc Slonim, *Modern Russian Literature, from Chekhov to the Present*, p. 214.

reading of certain poems when we approach them with these precepts in mind. But I must first say something of a critic who has been before me in applying Fenollosa's speculations to the criticism of poetry.

Few people have looked at Fenollosa and those who have, have seen him through the spectacles of Ezra Pound. Pound has shown himself far more interested in Fenollosa's observations on the structure of words than in what he says about the structure of sentences. In Fenollosa's treatise these two bodies of reflections hang together, but it is possible, if one considers one without the other, to make them thrust against each other. Hence it comes about that Pound, who has done so much to dislocate and disrupt syntax in poetry, has been able, in doing so, to appeal to Fenollosa's authority. Fenollosa breaks down the Chinese ideogram for "red" into "Rose: Iron Rust: Cherry: Flamingo". And he puts this forward as the product of a way of thinking preferable to our way of abstraction, which explains red as colour, colour as vibration, vibration as a mode of energy, and so on, moving ever further away from the perception of concreteness. But Fenollosa never suggests that this way of thinking is preferable to the way of thinking that produces the sentence. Quite the contrary: Fenollosa values as highly the way of thinking by sentences as the way of thinking by ideogram. He holds up Chinese as a model, because in that language the two ways of thinking work together. Pound, on the other hand, attempts to substitute thinking by ideogram for thinking by sentences; and the work of articulation that is done by syntax he hands over, in his own poetry, to the element of rhythm (in its widest sense). Hence it comes about that so long as we see Fenollosa only in Pound's terms, we only squint at him.

I find this squint in the work of Hugh Kenner.[1] Mr. Kenner is at his best in his chapter on "The Moving Image". When he comes to ideogram, to which he gives much fuller attention, he draws out a central thread in Fenollosa's thought, the Aristo-

[1] Hugh Kenner, *The Poetry of Ezra Pound.*

40

telean doctrine of *mimesis*, especially as it is related to the Aristotelean encomium of metaphor:

> Metaphor, as Aristotle tells us in another place, affirms that four things (*not* two) are so related that A is to B as C is to D. When we say "The ship ploughs the waves", we aren't calling a ship a plough. We are intuitively perceiving the similarity in two dissimilar actions: "The ship does to the waves what a plough does to the ground."[1]

As Mr. Kenner rightly says, this is at odds with our common conception of metaphor as combining only two terms, "tenor" and "vehicle". But already the critic contradicts himself. As he says, "We are intuitively perceiving the similarity in two dissimilar actions." Yet when he contends that metaphor relates four things rather than two, it is precisely this similarity that is scanted. The metaphor relates not two things, nor four either, but six: the plough, the ship, the ground, the waves, *the action of ploughing, the action of sailing*. Fenollosa, who insists so loudly on the importance of verbs, and the distinctions between them, is here called in to justify a view of metaphor which reduces all transitive verbs to a colourless "doing to".

The consequences of this appear when Mr. Kenner considers a poem two lines long:

> Swiftly the years beyond recall.
> Solemn the stillness of this spring morning.

He comments:

> Two experiences, two concretions of emotion, are juxtaposed to yield the proportion, "My feelings of transience are held in tension with my desire to linger amid present pleasures, as the flight of time is in tension with the loveliness of this spring morning." The presence of two purely emotional components among the requisite four does not differentiate this in principle from the entirely "objective" metaphor, "The ship ploughs the waves."[2]

[1] Hugh Kenner, *op. cit.*, p. 87.
[2] *Ibid.*, p. 90.

No; but the absence of two components out of the requisite six—this does make a difference. What are missing are the verbs, hence the syntax. Where the verbs should be, the ploughing or the sailing, we have only the yawning vagueness of "held in tension with". Significantly what we get is only a state, an immobile grouping, not an action, a dynamic transference of energy. As Mr. Kenner says, "The Chinese ideograph . . . deals in exceedingly condensed juxtapositions." And in this he says it is "like the metaphor". But on Fenollosa's showing, the Chinese sentence does not "deal in juxtapositions", any more than the English sentence does. It does not just put things together, it moves from one to another, knitting webs of force. And if Aristotle's example is to be taken as the type of the metaphor, then it seems to resemble the sentence more than the ideograph.

V

SYNTAX AS ACTION IN SIDNEY,
SHAKESPEARE, AND OTHERS

❧❧❧❧❧❧❧❧❧❧❧❧❧❧❧❧❧❧❧❧❧❧❧❧❧❧❧❧❧❧❧

WHAT happens if we read some well-known poems
Fenollosa's injunctions in mind? It is worth stopping
to see, but to be fair to Fenollosa, we ought to
realize that the exercise is purely experimental. We read in this
way simply to see what happens, what conclusions we are led
to about the value of the poems in question. The question
whether we endorse these conclusions or reject them shall for
the moment be waived altogether.

I have chosen for the purpose a group of poems, or passages
of poetry, mostly from the sixteenth century and mostly about
sleep. The first of them is a famous sonnet by Sidney:

> Come, Sleep! O sleep, the certain knot of peace,
> The baiting-place of wit, the balm of woe,
> The poor man's wealth, the prisoner's release,
> The indifferent judge between the high and low;
> With shield of proof shield me from out the press
> Of those fierce darts Despair at me doth throw:
> O make in me these civil wars to cease;
> I will good tribute pay if thou do so.
> Take thou of me smooth pillows, sweetest bed,
> A chamber deaf to noise and blind to light,
> A rosy garland and a weary head.

43

> And if these things, as being thine in right,
> Move not thy heavy grace, thou shalt in me,
> Livelier than elsewhere, Stella's image see.

According to Fenollosa, the natural norm for syntax, and hence the poetic ideal, is: *term from which→transference of force→ term to which*; or, *agent→act→object*. Of this there is hardly anything in Sidney's poem; where such straightforward transference of energy is in sight, Sidney avoids it by juggling with word-order—"I will good tribute pay". The imperative or permissive verbal forms, however natural to the invocation, do not conform to this pattern; and the pervasive grammatical device is the arrangement of the catalogue, of phrases connected only by commas, each standing for the mere copula.

Sleep does not, as with Shakespeare, "knit up the ravelled sleeve of care"; it simply *is* "the certain knot of peace". The sense, we may say, is the same, but in Shakespeare the force is transferred temporally through the transitive verb; Sidney's copula evades the transference of energy, and is static, asserting an equivalence, where Shakespeare's verb is dynamic, an imitation of action. In the same way, Sidney's sleep does not "bait"; it is a baiting-place. It does not soothe; it is not even "a soothing", but a balm. It does not enrich the poor man; it is not even "his riches", but his wealth. It does not free the prisoner; it is his release. It does not judge; it *is* a judge.

Fenollosa would economize on prepositions, but Sidney dwells on them: not "from", but "from out the press of". "Press" to mean "throng" is a noun Fenollosa should admire, for it incorporates much verbal energy; but in applying it to darts Sidney applies the word to just that kind of throng, a flying cloud, where its verbal force is unacceptable and has to be suppressed by the reader from his attention.

"Smooth pillows", "sweetest bed", "chamber", "garland", and "weary head" repeat the merely copulative arrangement of the first lines—but with a difference. Fenollosa had written of "the tyranny of mediaeval logic":

44

According to this European logic, thought is a kind of brick-yard. It is baked into little hard units or concepts. These are piled in rows according to size and then labelled with words for future use. This use consists in picking out a few bricks, each by its convenient label, and sticking them together into a sort of wall called a sentence by the use either of white mortar for the positive copula "is", or of black mortar for the negative copula "is not". In this way we produce such admirable propositions as "A ring-tailed baboon is not a constitutional assembly".

Let us consider a row of cherry trees. From each of these in turn we proceed to take an "abstract", as the phrase is, a certain common lump of qualities which we may express together by the name cherry or cherry-ness. Next we place in a second table several such characteristic concepts: cherry, rose, sunset, iron-rust, flamingo. From these we abstract some further common quality, dilutation or mediocrity, and label it "red" or "red-ness". It is evident that this process of abstraction may be carried on indefinitely and with all sorts of material. We may go on for ever building pyramids of attenuated concept until we reach the apex "being".

But we have done enough to illustrate the characteristic pro-cess. At the base of the pyramid lie *things*, but stunned, as it were. They can never know themselves for things until they pass up and down among the layers of the pyramids. The way of passing up and down the pyramid may be exemplified as follows: we take a concept of lower attenuation, such as "cherry"; we see that it is contained under one higher, such as "redness". Then we are permitted to say in sentence form, "Cherryness is contained under redness", or for short, "(The) cherry is red". If, on the other hand, we do not find our chosen subject under a given predicate we use the black copula and say, for example, "(The) cherry is not liquid".

Now it is plain that Sidney's "smooth pillows", his "sweetest bed", and the rest are things which, in Fenollosa's vivid phrase, have been "stunned". They are not metaphors for sleep, nor, in any precise sense, symbols of sleep; they are particulars of the abstraction sleep. And it is natural to connect this with the role of the mistress in the Petrarchan sonnet. The mistress of the Petrarchan or Platonic love-poet is, through a sonnet-sequence, stunned time and again, attenuated more and more, until all that is left of her is an abstract "worthiness". Sometimes, when the poet complains of her cruelty, she is abstracted further still, into the ultimate abstraction "being". What began as a living woman is squeezed out until it is a pin-point target for the lover's will.

Altogether, it seems indisputable that Sidney's poem, under Fenollosa's scrutiny, will come off very badly indeed. It is poetry where the verb is evaded whenever possible.

§ 2

A poem of roughly the same period as Sidney's and on the same subject is Daniel's "Care-charmer Sleep". This too begins with a clutter of phrases in opposition, apparently simple copulas:

> Care-charmer Sleep, son of the sable Night,
> Brother to death . . .

But this is different from anything in Sidney's poem. Sleep, Night, and Death are not particulars of one stunning abstraction. Nor, on the other hand, is Sleep going to do anything to Night or to Death, as Sidney's sleep was going to knot peace and bait wit, until prevented by having its verbs wrenched from it one by one. There is no conceivable verb that could convey the relation of Sleep to Night, or of Sleep to Death. Yet these relationships are being established, by the copulas understood and the metaphor (not a very lively one) of family kinship. The relationship established is a correspondence, not an equivalence. Night is the sleep of the world; death is the sleep of the soul. Articulation is effected, but no force is expended, for none is needed.

Fenollosa had declared that "thought is successive . . . because the operations of nature are successive." But these lines belie him. This is a sort of thought that does not go by sequence in time; if it did, it could be expressed in sentences. Daniel starts

46

with Sleep and goes on to Night and Death, but he could equally well have started with Night or with Death (as other poets did), for in fact the three things come together. When we talk about this sort of thing we use a metaphor from space, not from time: Sleep corresponds, *on one level*, to Death *on another level*. Yet this too is only a makeshift. As Bergson says, "We think in terms of space—the insurmountable difficulties presented by certain philosophic problems arise from the fact that we separate out in space, phenomena which do not occupy space." And the poet himself needs no spatial metaphors. What we have to deal with, in fact, is articulation not by syntax, neither narrative syntax like Fenollosa's, nor the propositional syntax of the logician, but by dream or myth, alogical and mysterious. It is plain that the sentence, "Death is sleepy", though propositional in form, is not a true proposition, which can be achieved by running up and down Fenollosa's pyramids. On the other hand it cannot be transformed into the narrative sentence that Fenollosa asks for, transmitting energy through a transitive verb. It seems, therefore, that the copula, in a sentence of this sort, does not deserve the opprobrium that Fenollosa heaps on it—unless, of course, one describes the statement, and Daniel's verses, as nonsense; in which case a lot of similar statements, from verse of all periods, must go through the window after it.

It is well established that a great deal of Elizabethan thought was of this kind, perceiving correspondences on different "levels". This thing on one level corresponds to that thing on another, level above level, microcosm inside macrocosm, sphere outside sphere. It often seems there is no movement in "the Elizabethan world-picture"; or what movement there is, is movement that cancels itself out, like the dance in which the dancer ends where he started, or the circular motion of the sphere which returns upon itself. It was an age that appreciated Spenser's ingenious and radical dislocation of narrative order in *The Faerie Queen*. The timeless and motionless painted emblem, or the dance in which time and motion abrogate

47

themselves, seem to be better media than language for expressing some characteristically Elizabethan attitudes. Certainly, if one accepts Fenollosa's version of the functions of language and syntax in poetry, that is the conclusion one is forced to. According to Fenollosa, a verb denotes the action of a mind or a body or a force, in time. If one believes that significant action occurs outside the dimension of time ("reality" being "timeless"), and that the significant acts of the mind, those by which it apprehends reality, are escapes out of time into eternity, one's use of language will obviously not conform to Fenollosa's pattern.

This is the case for instance with a genuinely mystical poet like Henry Vaughan:

> Dear Night! this world's defeat;
> The stop to busy fools; care's check and curb;
> The day of spirits; my soul's calm retreat
>   Which none disturb!
> Christ's progress, and His prayer-time;
> The hours to which high Heaven doth chime.
>
> God's silent, searching flight;
> When my Lord's head is filled with dew, and all
> His locks are wet with the clear drops of night;
>   His still, soft call;
> His knocking time; the soul's dumb watch,
>   When spirits their fair kindred catch.

This begins with copulas like Sidney's and proceeds to copulas like Daniel's; and it is essential to the persuasive effect that the syntactical form should be the same throughout. Night is "care's check and curb" as Sleep is "the baiting-place of wit". But Night is not *the time of* God's flight; it *is* that flight, by the same dream-logic that produced for Daniel, "Sleep is the brother of Death". And for Vaughan as for Daniel, the syntactical form of *the sentence* is out of the question. This admitted, the poem answers Fenollosa's prescriptions very well. Far more than Sidney, Vaughan uses nouns full of verbal energy, "stop", "check", "curb", "watch". In this way he expends great

48

positive energy in expressing negations. To quote Fenollosa, "all apparently negative or disruptive movements bring into play other positive forces. It requires great effort to annihilate."

§ 3

Our next example shall be from Shakespeare. Fenollosa observed:

> I have seldom seen our rhetoricians dwell on the fact that the great strength of our language lies in its splendid array of transitive verbs, drawn both from Anglo-Saxon and from Latin sources. These give us the most individual characterizations of force. Their power lies in their recognition of nature as a vast storehouse of forces. We do not say in English that things seem, or appear, or eventuate, or even that they are; but that they *do*. Will is the foundation of our speech. We catch the Demi-urge in the act. I had to discover for myself why Shakespeare's English was so immeasurably superior to all others. I found that it was his persistent, natural, and magnificent use of hundreds of transitive verbs. Rarely will you find an "is" in his sentences. "Is" weakly lends itself to the uses of our rhythm, in the unaccented syllables; yet he sternly discards it. A study of Shakespeare's verbs should underlie all exercises in style.

Plainly Fenollosa chooses Shakespeare as the case on which his argument may rest. Shakespeare should bear him out, if any can:

O sleep! O gentle sleep!
Nature's soft nurse, how have I frighted thee,
That thou no more wilt weigh my eyelids down
And steep my senses in forgetfulness?
Why rather, sleep, liest thou in smoky cribs
Upon uneasy pallets stretching thee,
And hushed with buzzing night-flies to thy slumber,
Than in the perfumed chambers of the great,
Under the canopies of costly state,
And lulled with sound of sweetest melody?
O thou dull god! why liest thou with the vile

49

> In loathsome beds, and leav'st the kingly couch
> A watch-case or a common 'larum bell?
> Wilt thou upon the high and giddy mast
> Seal up the ship-boy's eyes, and rock his brains
> In cradle of the rude imperious surge,
> And in the visitation of the winds,
> Who take the ruffian billows by the top,
> Curling their monstrous heads, and hanging them
> With deafening clamour in the slippery clouds,
> That with the hurly death itself awakes?
> Canst thou, O partial sleep! give thy repose
> To the wet sea-boy in an hour so rude,
> And in the calmest and most stillest night,
> With all appliances and means to boot,
> Deny it to a King? Then, happy low, lie down!
> Uneasy lies the head that wears a crown.

Shakespeare begins, like Sidney and Daniel with a phrase in opposition, a copula. Sleep is "Nature's soft nurse". But the stock correspondence (Sleep = Death) is held in abeyance through many lines, and when it comes, it is as paradox and hyperbole—"That with the hurly death itself awakes". The lines are full of energy. Sleep, the negation of activity, is presented as supremely active. ("It requires great effort to annihilate.") So Sleep weighs eyelids, steeps senses, seals eyes, and rocks brains. The word "leav'st" transfers energy to three things at once, to the King's couch, the watch-case, and the 'larum bell. This ability to affect at once things so widely different quite belies the not very energetic sense of the word in common usage, and makes "leaving" a very positive action indeed. Moreover, this energy is noisy; this is the pervasive paradox by which sleep is invoked in lines which crash and reverberate with the tolling of bells, the ticking of watches, the buzzing of flies, the clamour and hurly-burly of a storm at sea.

The whole drift of the passage, its literal sense and its metaphorical effect, is towards denying what Sidney took for granted, that a certain range of things are particulars which may

stand for "sleep", the abstraction—pillows, for instance, gar-
lands, and beds. Once sleep is seen, as Shakespeare sees it,
to be an energy, then it is seen more truly in terms of the most
refractory things on which that energy plays, or (more truly
still) in verbs which denote the ways that energy expends itself.

Thus Shakespeare does all that Fenollosa says. He bears him
out completely. And yet there are, even here, syntactical
elements for which Fenollosa makes no provision. There is for
instance the chain of interrogations. As we have seen and as
Fenollosa led us to expect, each bloc of verse that concludes
with a question-mark has the force not of an interrogation,
but of a narrative statement. What we take in, as we hear these
lines declaimed from the stage, is a series of moving images,
little narratives. We watch sleep doing things; we do not
enquire, as the question-marks suggest that we do, why sleep
refuses to do these things in the presented instance. These are,
as we say, rhetorical questions. That is to say, the interrogative
forms are the empty or emptied forms of a pseudo-syntax. The
true syntax is narrative; only the pseudo-syntax is interrogative. It is significant that we should call such pseudo-questions
"rhetorical". As we shall see, rhetoric is traditionally the province of pseudo-syntax; our expression, "rhetorical question",
testifies to our acknowledgment of that.

The last of the questions is, or may be different. The King
may pause after it, enquiring of his own state of mind, "Is it
true I am to get no sleep tonight? Am I in the least sleepy?" No,
he realizes, he is not; and yes, sleep can deny itself to him. So
the question is answered, and he heaves himself out of bed
with:

Uneasy lies the head that wears a crown.

If the episode is acted in this way, then the last question is a
true question, not, like those before it, the repetition and varia-
tion of a rhythmical pattern, or so many screws to press up the
tension of the hearer. In this way, the last question is not a
rhetorical question, because it waits upon an answer. And its
interrogative syntax is authentic. It must be so, I think, and

this must be the correct way of playing it, because the language is different from that of the questions that precede it. Gone are the concretions. Instead, "an hour so rude", "the calmest and most stillest night", "with all appliances and means to boot"— the language is abstract and generalized.

Again, "Uneasy lies the head that wears a crown." Kings do not sleep in their crowns, and the image of their doing so is comical. Fortunately we are not in danger of making an image, because by this time the language has been let down so far from concreteness that we see the crown not as a thing at all, but as a symbol. Yet this is a sentence with a plot. Like Sackville's sentences about Camillus and Scipio, it changes direction dramatically on the relative pronoun, as does Cowper's couplet about the Israelites, where the relative pronoun is understood:

> And had the grace in scenes of peace to show
> The virtue they had learned in scenes of woe.

Shakespeare's line has gone over into the language as a maxim, like Chaucer's "high senténce", a meaning of "sentence" that Fenollosa might have done well to consider. If we cut out of poetry all statements such as this, because they are "abstractions", we cut away all that part of poetry that has gone into the store of folk-wisdom. The sentence enacts the thing it says, but not in any way that Fenollosa acknowledges.

§ 4

I cannot leave this excursion into sixteenth- and seventeenth-century poetry without pointing out that there are many poems of this period which lean on what Fenollosa calls "the discredited, or rather useless, logic of the Middle Ages", far more heavily and patently than even Sidney's sonnet on Sleep. An example is the same poet's "Because I oft in darke abstracted guise" (*Astrophel and Stella*, xxvii), which Miss Rosemond Tuve shows to be framed throughout on the pattern of a

Ramist argument. I can be brief here, for Miss Tuve has made the point at length. Such a poem, if we approach it from Fenollosa's point of view, offers us nothing whatever:

> It is necessary to get rid of the modern notion that "logic" in a poem will make it either coldly unimaginative or pedantically "abstract", if one is to notice without prejudice the relations between the poems these men wrote and the training they were given in logical invention.[1]

Miss Tuve asks us only "to notice without prejudice". To enjoy and respond is another matter again, and it is no good pretending that we can with ease persuade ourselves to respond to such movements of thought as "natural". On the other hand, there is evidence that they were natural enough to Sidney; and if we allow Fenollosa to persuade us there is only one "natural" movement of mind, we are blinded not only to the ways of thinking of the modern physicist, but to the ways of thinking of the Elizabethan gentleman. The loss may well be ours. I can just conceive, though I cannot share, a state of mind to which the turns and swerves of syntax in Sidney's sonnet would be as delightful and as meaningful as the turn on the pronoun in "Uneasy lies the head that wears a crown."

Astrophel and Stella, xxvii, is a pure example. Worse distortions occur in our reading when we come across logical syntax and abstractions in poems that, on other counts, we enjoy and want to admire. Then we either ignore the obtrusive logic, or we explain it away by supposing the poet's tone is ironical, so that he is mocking the logical syntax even as he uses it. (It is worth noting here that to the purist, wherever there is irony, there must be pseudo-syntax, because an ironical statement belies its own syntax, meaning something other than what the syntax says. The exaggerated value placed on irony in modern criticism is either a cause or a symptom of our dislike of authentic syntax in poetry.) Both these manœuvres occur in our reading of Donne. It has become a commonplace that

---

[1] Rosemond Tuve, *Elizabethan and Metaphysical Imagery*, p. 320.

Donne "exhibits a Shakespearean use of language", and this is true in many ways. Certainly it is true of Donne by contrast to Milton, and the comment was first made in the course of that comparison. But it is certainly not true if it is taken to mean that Donne works in terms of the moving image, as we have seen Shakespeare working in Henry IV's apostrophe to sleep. Much modern criticism of Donne takes "Shakespearean" in that sense. R. A. Brower, for instance, says of Donne's "Extasie", "certainly our sense of a finely ordered experience owes much to the clarity of this logical and dramatic design and to the fine tact with which it is expressed."[1] But that is as near as we get to any examination of Donne's syntax, and Mr. Brower goes on to extricate instead "the peculiar sequence of metaphors that make up its key design".

Fortunately I do not need to labour this point. Miss Tuve has been before me again, in showing how critics enamoured of the word as "thing" (and at this point Hulme and Fenollosa stand together) must distort Donne and Herbert no less than Sidney and Spenser:

> Donne is especially careful to indicate how we are to con-
> ceive the relation of smaller units to the structure of a whole.
> Such writing utilizes rather than avoids conceptual language.[2]

And again, discussing Donne's statement of his poetic function as he conceives of it (at the end of the "Second Anniversary"):

> Like most Elizabethan comment, it asks us to read poems as
> though language were not a tool for announcing facts about a
> particular *thou* or *I* in their character of particular phenomena,
> but a medium for intimating and ordering significances which
> particulars shadow forth.[3]

There is no need to point out that, if this element is to be found in Donne, Fenollosa could only turn down his thumbs.

[1] R. A. Brower, *The Fields of Light*, p. 80.
[2] Tuve, *op. cit.*, p. 178.
[3] *Ibid.*, p. 179.

§ 5

Enough has been said to show that if we take Fenollosa seriously, we shall find ourselves rejecting as "unpoetic" the greater part of what has been most admired in the poetry of the sixteenth and seventeenth centuries. This is something not much short of a *reductio ad absurdum*. Yet Fenollosa's success with Shakespeare suggests that his views are not so much incorrect as incomplete. And the impression of solitary originality remains; for Fenollosa puts into our hands a wholly new technique, and in some cases it pays enormous dividends. No one before Fenollosa looked at Shakespeare as he has done, and Shakespeare, looked at in this way, shines out magnificently alive.

VI

SYNTAX AS ACTION IN EIGHTEENTH-CENTURY POETIC THEORY

To recapitulate: Hulme would banish syntax from poetry; Mrs. Langer would banish it but would retain its forms while perverting their function, so as to make syntax into music; only Fenollosa would retain syntax and set great store by it. Does he stand quite alone in this? So far as I can see, in his own age and ever since, he does. But I have remarked that the temper of his mind was Augustan. Is there, then, in Augustan criticism a theory of poetic syntax which does not make syntax into music?

There is. It is the tradition of "the strength of Denham". When Pope exhorts his readers to

> praise the easy vigour of a line
> Where Denham's strength and Waller's sweetness join,

few of them nowadays understand what he means. With "vigour" for a clue, most of them will suppose that Pope meant by "strength" what Jeffrey meant, when he said of the "very sweet verses" of Samuel Rogers:

> They do not, indeed, stir the spirit like the strong lines of Byron, nor make our hearts dance within us, like the inspiring strains of Scott.[1]

[1] *Essays from "The Edinburgh Review"*, ed. Bennett (1924), p. 112.

But no one could call Denham's poetry stirring, and Jeffrey, when he distinguishes the sweetness of Rogers from the strength of Byron, does not mean quite the same as Pope does when he distinguishes the sweetness of Waller from the strength of Denham. In the criticism of the eighteenth century, "strength" has nothing to do with ardour or emotional pressure; it goes along with "sense":

> Our great Forefathers in Poetic Song
> Were rude in Diction, tho' their sense was Strong...[1]

> Unpolish'd Beauties grac'd the artless Song,
> Tho' rude the diction, yet the Sense was Strong...[2]

... we may still discern that his sense was strong, and his wit genuine.[3]

Certainly, if we try to distinguish in poetry between the sense of a passage and the feeling that informs it, we shall not get very far. Nevertheless there is obviously a difference, even when we talk of poetry, between strong feelings and strong sense. It is significant that "strong feelings" is still a normal expression in modern English, where "strong sense" is not. That in itself suggests that we are dealing with something for which the name has been lost. So, too, perhaps has the relish for it, the capacity for enjoying or even for perceiving it. And in so far as we can distinguish between the sense of a poetic passage and its feeling, what we are looking for belongs to the first of these, to the conveying by poetry of paraphrasable meanings.

What must a poet do, then, in this part of his undertaking, to earn from an eighteenth-century critic the complimentary comment that "his sense was strong"? We go first to the fountainhead, to Denham himself:

[1] Jabez Hughes, *Upon reading Mr. Dryden's Fables* (c. 1707).
[2] Julia Madan (1721), quoted C. F. E. Spurgeon, 500 *Years of Chaucer Criticism*, I, 362.
[3] Robert Alves (1794), quoted Spurgeon, *op. cit.*, I, 495.

> Nor are the nerves of his compacted strength
> Stretched and dissolved into unsinewed length . . .[1]

The rhymes "strong/long" and "strength/length" become a commonplace:

> To mend one Fault, he makes a hundred more:
> A verse was weak, you turn it much too strong,
> And grow obscure, for fear you should be long . . .[2]

But this is more than a verbal tic, taken from the Rhyming Dictionary:

> . . . Virgil, who is all great and majestic etc., requires great strength of lines, weight of words, and closeness of expressions . . .[3]

> By striving to be short they grow Obscure;
> And when they would write smoothly they want
> Strength . . .[4]

> . . . illustration would impair the strength and render the sentiment too diffuse and languid . . .[5]

"Strong sense", we perceive, is "compacted" and "short". It requires "closeness of expressions". And it vanishes when expressions are too "long" and too "diffuse".

Examples could be multiplied. These should suffice to prove that "strength", as the eighteenth century understood it, was the ability to crowd much meaning into a short space. We may fairly assume that it is the ability manifested by Pope in his lines on Peterborough:

> And HE, whose lightning pierc'd th' Iberian Lines,
> Now forms my Quincunx, and now ranks my vines,
> Or tames the Genius of the stubborn plain,
> Almost as quickly as he conquer'd Spain.

[1] *To Sir Richard Fanshaw on his translation of Pastor Fido"* (1648).
[2] Ozell, *Boileau his Works made English* (1711).
[3] Milbourn (1698).
[4] Roscommon, *Ars Poetica* (c. 1690).
[5] John Newbery, *The Art of Poetry on a New Plan* (1762).

This is Sackville's Camillus and Scipio all over again, their rise and fall graphed, like Peterborough's, in the rush, the check, and the retreat of the sense through one rapid clause. This is narrative. No different in principle is the argumentative verse of the *Essay on Man*:

> Bring then these blessings to a strict account;
> Make fair deductions; see to what they mount;
> How much of other each is sure to cost;
> How each for other oft is wholly lost;
> How inconsistent greater goods with these;
> How sometimes life is risk'd, and always ease:
> Think, and if still the things thy envy call,
> Say, would'st thou be the Man to whom they fall?

This is the strength that resides in expressions which are "short", "compacted", "close". And this therefore is the poet who was welcomed:

> Hail Bard unequall'd in whose deathless line
> Reason and wit with strength collected shine:[1]

This is he of whom it is said, in the same poem:

> Each Roman's force adorns his various page;
> Gay smiles, collected strength, and manly rage.

"Collected" is another word to go with "compacted", "close".

But this, it may be thought, is nothing new. All critics in all ages have censured the poetry that is diffuse, or at least announced their preference for its opposite:

> The question of how concentrated a poem ought to be seems to me of the same order as how strong you like your tea. Along with most of my contemporaries I like it fairly strong; . . .[2]

Is not this modern critic's "strength" the same as Denham's, Roscommon's, Milbourn's, Julia Madan's? I think it is not. For

---

[1] Dr. John Brown, D.D., "On Satire", *Dodsley's Miscellany* (1745).
[2] Graham Hough, "The Scalpel and the Scales", *The Listener*, Aug. 28, 1952.

it is certainly true that most of us like the meanings of poetry to be "concentrated". But "concentration" is not necessarily "compactness" "Concentration" can come by many ways into poetry, down the avenues of dream, through the key-hole of innuendo, sidling through the false walls of irony, or shooting through a trapdoor from the cellarage of the unconscious. But none of these have much to do with "closeness of expressions", just as none of them have much to do with what has been quoted from Pope. "Strength", in other words, is close and compact syntax, neither more nor less.

And it is too a virtue of authentic syntax, not of the pseudo-syntax that is music. For a verse is strong only if it has "strong sense". Let syntax be never so close, unless it is truly carrying "weight of words", it cannot be "strong". To be "strong", poetic syntax must bind as well as join, not only gather together but fetter too. The actual function of meaning, "which calls for permanent contents", *must* be fulfilled. Verse may be "strong" or it may "aspire to the condition of music"; it cannot do both.

This "strength" hardly appears in nineteenth-century criticism. The word is used as frequently as ever, but it is much harder to be sure what it means. Maria Edgeworth writes in 1810:

> I do not like Lord Byron's *English Bards and Scotch Reviewers*, though, as my father says, the lines are very strong, and worthy of Pope and *The Dunciad*.[1]

This is probably strength as understood by Dryden and Johnson, not as understood by Jeffrey. And fifteen years later Miss Edgeworth was still using the old distinction between "strength" and "ease":

> You have probably seen in the papers the death of our admirable friend Mrs. Barbauld. I have copied for you her last letter to me and some beautiful lines written in her eightieth year. There is

[1] *Life and Letters of Maria Edgeworth*, ed. Augustus J. C. Hare, I, 172.

a melancholy elegance and force of thought in both. Elegance and strength—qualities rarely uniting without injury to each other—combine most perfectly in her style...[1]

So too in Crabbe, so often capable of admirably close syntax, it is not surprising to find a laboured imitation of Denham:

> Gay spite of time, though poor, yet well attired,
> Kind without love, and vain if not admir'd.[2]

This is meant to call to mind the hackneyed lines from *Cooper's Hill*, "which", says Johnson, "since Dryden has commended them, almost every writer for a century past has imitated". Obviously Crabbe knew the tradition, and was writing in it. But when *Blackwood's* in 1817 says of Byron, "strength, vigour, energy are his attributes", we no longer know whether this is the strength of Pope and Dryden, on the one hand, or of Jeffrey and Oliver Elton on the other.

And it is not surprising that just at this period the tradition should become hard to follow. As I shall suggest later, Coleridge is an authority more ambiguous than T. E. Hulme, for instance, realized. But we can agree with Sir Herbert Read[3] that once the idea of "organic form" was broached, poetic syntax began to move into the orbit of music and away from "strong sense". Wordsworth's revision of *The Prelude* is similarly, among other things, a movement from syntax to pseudo-syntax. And in fact the whole Romantic movement in poetry tended to minimize the responsibilities of poetry towards what the Augustan critics understood as "sense". Symbolism, from this point of view, only pushes to a logical extreme the implications of Romantic poetic theory. It was the Romantics who first suggested, by implication, that syntax could have only a phantasmal life in poetry.

Particularly interesting from this point of view are Byron

---

[1] *Life and Letters of Maria Edgeworth*, ed. Augustus J. C. Hare, II, 132.
[2] *The Borough* (1910), Letter xv.
[3] Sir Herbert Read, *The True Voice of Feeling*.

and Landor. Landor is the less important, but in all fairness his case must be mentioned, for his work represents one of the traps into which the pursuit of "strength", in the old sense, could lead the poet. As late as 1863, Landor was writing:

> Poets as strong as ever were
> Formerly breath'd our British air:
> Ours now display but boyish strength,
> And rather throw themselves full length.
> Waller was easy, so was Sedley,
> Nor mingled with the rhyming medley . . .[1]

These wretched verses are one among many examples of the importance for Landor of the old distinction between "strength" and "ease". Yet the merest glance at any of Landor's heroic poems will show that he achieved close syntax indeed, but at an exorbitant cost. For his is not after all the strength of Denham, of Pope, of Crabbe, but the strength of Milton. In order to get syntactical closeness, Landor treats the English language as if it were Latin. And even if we make Milton himself a special case, it must be admitted as a rule that "strength" is not worth this sort of sacrifice. Nevertheless in Landor can be found at times something approaching Pope's "thriving plants ignoble broomsticks made", that "sweep those Alleys they were born to shade". The fate of Goliath is mirrored, though clumsily, in syntax:

> From the brook,
> Striking another such, another day,
> A little pebble stretcht the enormous bulk
> That would have fill'd it and have turned its course.[2]

Byron is the crucial case. Byron is "strong", so everyone in his own day agreed. But he is strong in both ways, in the Augustan way and the Romantic; so when Jeffrey says that Byron is "strong", and when Richard Lovell Edgeworth says so, they do not mean the same thing. The shift of meaning in

---

[1] *Poetical Works*, ed. Wheeler (Oxford), II, 439.
[2] *The Siege of Ancona*, Act IV, Sc. 2.

the term is nowhere so clear as when different comments on Byron's verse are set side by side. Accordingly, in Byron syntax turns into pseudo-syntax before our eyes. His housemaid who has risen in the world "dines from off the plate she lately wash'd" and "rules the circle which she served before". But, turned a governess, she finds her charge too innately good for her to spoil:

> Foil'd was perversion by that youthful mind,
> Which Flattery fool'd not, Baseness could not blind,
> Deceit infect not, near Contagion soil,
> Indulgence weaken, nor Example spoil,
> Nor master'd Science tempt her to look down
> On humbler talents with a pitying frown,
> Nor Genius swell, nor Beauty render vain,
> Nor Envy ruffle to retaliate pain,
> Nor Fortune change, Pride raise, nor Passion bow,
> Nor virtue teach austerity—till now.[1]

The little rhythm, common in Pope and inherent in a common syntactical arrangement, grows more and more emphatic as sound usurps sense, or as sound drags the sense behind it, until it rises to a crescendo and a roll of drums "—till now". What began as syntax has become music—not, as it happens, very subtle music, but that is beside the point.

A truly learned critic, no doubt, could write the full history of poetic syntax in English, a history to which I have contributed here no more than the sketch of a single chapter. But the point I want to make is this: in the seventeenth and eighteenth centuries poets acted on the assumption that syntax in poetry should often, if not always, carry a weight of poetic meaning; in the nineteenth and twentieth centuries poets have acted on the opposite assumption, that when syntactical forms are retained in poetry those forms can carry no weight. I have sought only to make these assumptions explicit, so that we may know just what we are doing, and what we are turning our backs upon,

[1] *A Sketch* (1816)

63

when we agree with the symbolists that in poetry syntax turns into music. Is Pope's handling of poetic syntax really so irrelevant to the writing of poetry today? And are we really so sure of ourselves that we can afford to break so completely with the tradition he represents?

VII

VARIETIES OF POETIC SYNTAX

❧❧❧❧❧❧❧❧❧❧❧❧❧❧❧❧❧❧❧❧❧❧❧❧❧❧❧❧❧❧

1. INTRODUCTION. GRAMMAR AND LOGIC

I A. RICHARDS maintains[1] that grammar often violates logic. In this he challenges J. S. Mill who held that it does not. Richards points out:

> "Socrates is wise,
>   Wisdom belongs to Socrates
> are two different word-patterns; the same form of thought might use either."

But the only "forms of thought" that Richards recognizes are those of logic. And it may be true that what is the same form of thought to the logician may divide into two quite distinct "forms of thought" for the poet. It is not hard to imagine poetic contexts in which one of the word-patterns about Socrates might recommend itself to the poet where the other wouldn't. In such a case, the poet would find himself siding with the grammarian against the logician.

This possibility of setting grammarian and logician at odds is seldom realized by apologists for poetry. A good example of this is T. E. Hulme, who implies that since poetry is illogical in its methods, it is therefore ungrammatical, in particular non-syntactical.

On the other hand, this point was well taken by Ernest

[1] *Interpretation in Teaching*, pp. 284, 285.

Fenollosa, who unfortunately has been much less influential than Hulme on later literary criticism. He puts poet with grammarian, as against logician. It is true, however, that the ally he seeks for the poet is an ideal grammarian who has broken for good the alliance with logic. Moreover, Fenollosa is not interested in "forms of thought", or rather he is interested in "forms of thought" only where they parallel forms of non-mental existence. Such are, he maintains, the forms of thought truly apparent in grammar as it has organically developed, though this cosmic sanction for grammatical forms has been consistently obscured by grammarians who will not break from the leading-strings of logic.

Fenollosa thus takes the forms of grammar very seriously; Hulme takes them seriously enough to want to debar them from poetry as seriously pernicious. Far more common is the view that they are not serious at all, and therefore that the poet may retain them or abjure them as he chooses. Suzanne Langer and most symbolist theorists think he might as well maintain them, since he can use them for his own purposes, which are not, however, those of the grammarians. He can make music out of them.

We have to agree that the forms of grammar certainly can be used in this way by the poet; and we owe a great deal to the symbolist theorists, and to a post-symbolist like Mrs. Langer, for making us aware of this resource available to the poet. For it illuminates some effects achieved, not only by symbolist and post-symbolist poets, but by many pre-symbolists also. On the other hand, there is a limit to this kind of thing; some poets retain the forms of grammar while emptying them of their articulating function, and yet do not provide articulation of any other kind. This seems to me vicious, for here syntax has been perverted to no end. We have lost the syntax, and got no music in exchange.

But I am particularly concerned to rebut those critics who, proceeding from a position like Mrs. Langer's, assume that whenever traditional syntactical forms appear in poetry, they are *necessarily* emptied of their grammatical function, *inevitably* less than serious, a phantasmal play on the surface of the poem. "Syntax as music" explains much; it does not explain all the parts that syntax may play in building up poetic effect. More apposite to some kinds of poetry is Fenollosa's view that the syntax of the transitive sentence obeys a law of nature. Or again, in other kinds of poetry, syntax renders a "form of thought" more faithfully than the logican does, and with a flexibility that Fenollosa did not dream of.

In fact, I distinguish five kinds of poetic syntax, as follows: (i) subjective, (ii) dramatic, (iii) objective, (iv) syntax like music, (v) syntax like mathematics. But before I go on, I had better define at this point what I mean by "poetic syntax". When we speak of "poetic imagery", we do not usually mean "all imagery that appears in poetry"; we even allow that "poetic imagery" can occur in prose. It is just the same with my "poetic syntax"; and if I take my examples mainly from poetry, that is merely to suit my own convenience.

Most people, if they think about the syntax of poetry at all, regard it as something neutral, in itself neither favourable nor unfavourable to poetry, a mere skeleton on which are hung the truly poetic elements, such as imagery or rhythm. Even when syntactical neatness is acknowledged as giving pleasure, there is a reluctance about admitting that this pleasure is poetic. But a skeleton obviously has a great deal to do with the beauty or ugliness of the body it supports. And, in fact, on second thoughts we may wonder whether the syntax of poetry can ever be aesthetically neutral, a matter of indifference. It can, however. It can be unremarkable, like a human frame that is neither close-knit nor loose-limbed, neither well- nor ill-proportioned, but just normal. Much syntax in poetry is of this kind, and is therefore not poetic syntax as I understand it. For that matter, poetry, it seems, can be invertebrate, as at the end of *The Waste Land* or in much of Pound's *Cantos*, where the poet does without not just conventional syntax but any syntax at all—though never, I think, without loss.

For my own part I affirm that syntax in poetry can be itself a source of poetic pleasure. And it is only to distinguish between the several pleasures it can give, and not (perish the thought) in hopes of furnishing a new gleaming piece of critical machinery, that I have put forward provisionally the fivefold classification which I now want to explain and develop.

2. SUBJECTIVE SYNTAX

Poetic syntax is *subjective* when its function is to please us by the fidelity with which it follows the "form of thought" in the poet's mind. There has recently appeared an admirable poem by Robert Graves which drives this point home because it pushes this capability of poetic syntax to an extreme. The piece is in fact a *tour-de-force*:

LEAVING THE REST UNSAID

Finis, apparent on an earlier page,
With fallen obelisk for colophon,
Must this be here repeated?

Death has been ruefully announced
And to die once is death enough,
Be sure, for any lifetime.

Must the book end, as you would end it,
With testamentary appendices
And graveyard indices?

But no, I will not lay me down
To let your tearful music mar
The decent mystery of my progress.

So now, my solemn ones, leaving the rest unsaid,
Rising in air as on a gander's wings
At a careless comma,

There is surely no need to labour the point that the handling of syntax here is a main source of the pleasure we get from the poem. Once we have taken this point, we are in a position to appreciate poetic syntax where its effect is similar but less obtrusive and, just for that reason perhaps, more powerful, as at the beginning of Coleridge's "Dejection":

> Well! If the Bard was weather-wise, who made
>   The grand old ballad of Sir Patrick Spence,
> This night, so tranquil now, will not go hence
> Unroused by winds that ply a busier trade
> Than those which mould yon cloud in lazy flakes,
> Or the dull sobbing draft, that moans and rakes
> Upon the strings of this Aeolian lute,
>   Which better far were mute.

These eight lines slide down a long scale of emotion from something not far short of geniality to a desperate melancholy; this rapid transition is affecting and compelling just because it is all done in the compass of a single complex sentence. And we are sobered and shocked when the mood reaches rock-bottom just because this is acknowledged in a last subordinate clause, as an afterthought, almost under the breath. It is this syntactical arrangement that conveys the poignant impression that this last admission has been wrung out of the poet unwillingly, as if he has said more than he meant to say, having started (this is now the effect of the first two lines) with a determination to keep up appearances.

Obviously, when syntax can do so much as this, it is rendering far more than "the form of thought" as Richards and the logicians conceive of it. In fact, if we are to retain that expression—"form of thought"—at all, we must take "thought" in the very loose sense it always has when we talk of "poetic thought" in general; what is being rendered to us is a form of *experience*, from which "thought" in the logician's sense is an abstraction. Here already the poet stands with the grammarian against the logician.

We see this very clearly when we find a poet making play with just those discrepancies between grammar and logic to which Richards draws attention. Richards points out that there are often two or more forms of grammar to render what the logician recognizes as one form of thought; he also points out (and draws upon Jespersen, in doing so) that the opposite case also occurs, where there is available only one form of grammar to cover what the logician sees as many different forms of thought. A good example of a poet exploiting this discrepancy, driving a wedge between grammar and logic, is the attack "On the Lord Chancellor Hyde", a poem attributed sometimes to Rochester, sometimes to Charles II:

> Pride, Lust, Ambition, and the People's Hate,
> The Kingdom's Broker, Ruin of the State,
> Dunkirk's sad loss, Divider of the Fleet,
> Tangier's Compounder for a barren Sheet: . . .

Here the play is all on the ambiguity of the possessive case in English, as in that detective-story, "The Murder of my Aunt", where the murder turns out to belong to the aunt because she committed it, not because she suffered it. So here, the hate belongs to the people because they direct it on Hyde, but also to Hyde because he suffers it; on the other hand, the ruin belongs to the state because the state suffers it, but it belongs to Hyde because he is responsible for it. The loss belongs to Dunkirk, because Dunkirk suffered it, being lost to England when Hyde sold it to France; it belongs to Hyde because, having sold it, "that was his loss"; Dunkirk has lost Hyde because he is an English subject and she is no longer part of England, but then Hyde is "no loss" to anyone or anything (and therefore "*sad* loss" is sarcastic); finally, when Dunkirk was sold, that was England's loss, yet also Hyde's because the loss was *his* doing. "Tangier's compounder" is more complicated still. Admittedly here the very elaboration of the device takes us a long way from the seriousness of Coleridge; yet the one possessive form, it could be argued, is true to "the form of thought", in that Hyde is seen throughout as never in possession of himself, but always a tool, in the pay or in the power of some person or institution. He plays a different part in each of the situations here glanced at, and in many of those situations he played a disastrously active role, yet (so the construction suggests) he was never in command of any situation, but commanded by it. In the specially abusive seventeenth-century sense he was always someone's or something's "creature", just as every peerage is some monarch's "creation"; and the poet goes on, in fact, to call him "a shrub of gentry", an upstart who can be uprooted as easily as he was planted.

This example from the Restoration period has to do with grammar, but not, strictly speaking, with syntax. For a further instance consider:

> Wandering lonely as a cloud
> That floats on high o'er vales and hills,
> All at once I saw a crowd,
> A host of golden daffodils;
> Beside the lake, beneath the trees,
> Fluttering and dancing in the breeze.

Is there not here an unmistakable loss of poetic pressure? Yet the changes I have introduced—"Wandering", for "I wandered", and the omission of "When" at the start of line three—are surely too slight to account for this loss on the scores of euphony and/or rhythm. The changes made are radical only in one respect, as regards syntax. To make the seeing and not the wandering the main clause of the sentence destroys the effect by which the daffodils, first seen in passing as the poet seems to turn away (his sentence completed, the daffodils acknowledged only in a subordinate clause), expand in unforeseen significance until the wandering mind is focused on them (the main clause forgotten, as the originally subordinate clause renews itself repeatedly in additional phrases). It is not that the poet sees more of the daffodils in a literal sense, catching sight of another bank of the flowers half-obscured by trees, but that he sees more *in* them, catching more and more of the powerful feeling and the significance that emanates from them.

71

A similar effect is developed on a larger scale by Coleridge in "This Lime-Tree Bower my Prison":

> Well, they are gone, and here must I remain,
> This lime-tree bower my prison! I have lost
> Beauties and feelings, such as would have been
> Most sweet to my remembrance even when age
> Had dimmed mine eyes to blindness! They, meanwhile,
> Friends, whom I never more may meet again,
> On springy heath, along the hill-top edge,
> Wander in gladness, and wind down, perchance,
> To that still roaring dell, of which I told;
> The roaring dell, o'erwooded, narrow, deep,
> And only speckled by the mid-day sun;
> Where its slim trunk the ash from rock to rock
> Flings arching like a bridge;—that branchless ash,
> Unsunned and damp, whose few poor yellow leaves
> Ne'er tremble in the gale, yet tremble still,
> Fanned by the water-fall! and there my friends
> Behold the dark green file of long lank weeds,
> That all at once (a most fantastic sight!)
> Still nod and drip beneath the dripping edge
> Of the blue claystone.

The last long sentence takes off from the "I have lost" of the one before. The poet defines this sense of loss by following in his imagination the friends he cannot accompany, whom he "never more may meet again", as they pass on to pleasures that he cannot share. But, just as in the Wordsworth stanza, this main statement, apparently completed, refuses to draw to a close, prolonging itself instead in subordinate constructions, each borrowing its impetus from the one before, the dell leading to the ash-tree, the tree through its tremulous leaves to the water-fall, and the water-fall through the water-weeds to "the blue clay-stone". When the poet thought all had been said, it turned out that nothing had been said; in calling to mind the pleasures he cannot share, his imagination permits him to share them. This refers back to the paradox which gives the poem its title. How can a bower of lime-trees be a prison? And, even as he begins to show how this can be, he proves that it cannot be, since the imagination cannot be imprisoned; and the poet goes on to acknowledge, at the end of the poem, that the prison is no prison, and the loss no loss. The syntax, continually finding new stores of energy where it has been affirmed that no more is to be found (the sentence, once the main verb has been introduced, seems ready to draw to a close), mimes, acts out in its own developing structure, the development of feeling behind it.

It is worthwhile to digress for a moment into prose-fiction and into a foreign language:

> Even the weather had obligingly accommodated itself to the setting: the day was neither bright nor gloomy but of a kind of bluey-grey tint such as is found only upon the worn-out uniforms of garrison soldiers, for the rest a peaceful class of warriors except for their being somewhat inebriate on Sundays.

This comes from Gogol's *Dead Souls*. And Vladimir Nabokov, in his brilliant book on Gogol, analyses it in terms which could be used, with minor modifications, of the sentence considered above from Coleridge:

> It is not easy to render the curves of this life-generating syntax in plain English so as to bridge the logical, or rather biological hiatus between a dim landscape under a dull sky and a groggy old soldier accosting the reader with a rich hiccup on the festive outskirts of the very same sentence. Gogol's trick consists in using as a link the word *"vprochem"* ("for the rest", "otherwise", *"d'ailleurs"*), which is a connection only in the grammatical sense but mimics a logical link, the word "soldiers" alone affording a faint pretext for the juxtaposition of "peaceful"; and as soon as this false bridge of *"vprochem"* has accomplished its magical work these mild warriors cross over, staggering and singing . . ."[1]

[1] Vladimir Nabokov, *Nikolai Gogol* (Editions Poetry, London, 1947), pp. 81, 82.

Here too, on Mr. Nabokov's showing, we see the poet siding with the grammarian against the logician. Of course, this sort of thing may be no more than a trick, an eccentric *tour-de-force*. Every time it occurs, whether in a poem or (at all frequently) in a novel, it has to be shown to be in accord with the burden of the whole. In Browning's "By the Fireside", for instance:

> —For the drop of the woodland fruit's begun,
> These early November hours,
>
> That crimson the creeper's leaf across
>   Like a splash of blood, intense, abrupt,
> O'er a shield else gold from rim to boss
>   And lay it for snow on the fairy-cupped
> Elf-needled mat of moss,
>
> By the rose-flesh mushrooms, undivulged
>   Last evening—nay, in today's first dew
> Yon sudden coral nipple bulged
>   Where a freaked, fawn-coloured, flaky crew
> Of toad-stools peep indulged.

Here, the toad-stools, the mushrooms, the moss, the shield, the creeper grow each out of the one before like Coleridge's water-weeds, his water-fall, and ash-tree, long after the main verb of the sentence ought to have spent its force. These forms of life in both poems, like the minor characters in Gogol's novel, "are engendered by the subordinate clauses of its various metaphors, comparisons and lyrical outbursts." But it is not at all so clear in Browning's baffling poem as in Coleridge's that this syntactical pattern acts out a train of feeling significant to the burden of the whole.

Further examples would be tedious. I will mention only:

> Surprised by joy—impatient as the Wind
> I turned to share the transport—oh! with whom
> But Thee, deep buried in the silent tomb,
> That spot which no vicissitude can find?

(Here certainly versification is very important, for the pauses at line-endings fall absolutely right. Still, the heart-breaking poignancy comes with the syntactical shift over from statement to question.) It will be remarked that this example comes from Wordsworth, and in fact, for illustrations of what I have called "subjective" syntax, I have drawn very heavily indeed on Wordsworth and Coleridge. I do not think this is mere coincidence. It is in these poets that I have found most often what I was looking for, and I am led to think that Sir Herbert Read, who also starts his search with these poets, may have been on the same trail when he sought "the true voice of feeling". If so, then he went wrong, I think, when he looked for "the true voice" in terms of the audible rhythms of versification rather than the inaudible rhythms of syntax. In that case he is right to insist upon blank-verse and free-verse as the natural vehicles of the true voice, but only because in those forms the articulations of rhythm can be broken down enough for the articulations of subjective syntax to take over.

This sort of poetic syntax, in fact, seems to me an aspect of what Coleridge and De Quincey call "eloquence", as distinct from "rhetoric"—a distinction, incidentally, which avoids the cruder, originally Platonic opposition between poetry and rhetoric, over which so many modern critics find themselves irreconcilably at loggerheads. De Quincey holds that both rhetoric and eloquence are or can be poetic, and that, although eloquence is superior, the one often shades into the other. And Coleridge remarks, "Eloquence itself—I speak of it as habitual and at call—too often is, and is always like to engender, a species of histrionism." He goes on to hope that he has avoided this histrionic shallowness of feeling, while yet rendering it with eloquence; and to give his grounds for hoping this. One of his reasons is as follows:

> . . . my eloquence was most commonly excited by the desire of running away and hiding myself from my personal and inward feelings, *and not for the expression of them*, while doubtless this very effort of feeling gave a passion and glow to my thoughts

and language on subjects of a general nature, that they otherwise would not have had. I fled in a Circle, still overtaken by the
Feelings, from which I was evermore fleeing, with my back
turned towards them; . . .

This fleeing in a circle, and being overtaken by the feelings
from which the poet flees, is just the pattern to be found in the
passage from "Dejection" and that from "This Lime-tree
Bower my Prison"; and in each case, even as this happens, the
syntax, assisted by but in command of the rhythm, acts it out
for the reader.

3. DRAMATIC SYNTAX

Poetic syntax is *dramatic* when its function is to please us by
the fidelity with which it follows the "form of thought" in
some mind other than the poet's, which the poet imagines.
This second kind of syntax is so obvious a corollary of the first
that it may seem pedantic to distinguish them. However, if I am
right, Wordsworth's passage beginning "Blest the babe", from
Book II of *The Prelude*, is dramatic in this way, and a critic so
scrupulous as Dr. Leavis, overlooking this, was led to misjudge
the poet's intentions.[1]

We should not suppose that the syntax of poetic drama is
always, in this sense, dramatic. Now that we no longer look at
each play by Shakespeare as a gallery of character-studies, we
no longer hear the claim made, that every figure in every play
is subtly differentiated by the rhythms and imagery of the
speeches put into his mouth. Even when Shakespeare plainly is
attempting to present a firmly delineated individual character,
such as Polonius, he still does so more by rhythm and imagery
than by syntax. Still syntax does play a part, as in the speech
on "Commodity" by the Bastard Faulconbridge, in *King
John* (Act II, Sc. 1):

> Mad world! mad Kings! mad composition!
> John, to stop Arthur's title in the whole,

[1]See *post*, pp. 106....116.

Hath willingly departed with a part:
And France, whose armour conscience buckled on,
Whom zeal and charity brought to the field
As God's own soldier, rounded in the ear
With that same purpose-changer, that sly devil,
That broker, that still breaks the pate of faith,
That daily break-vow, he that wins of all,
Of kings, of beggars, old men, young men, maids,
Who, having no external thing to lose
But the word "maid", cheats the poor maid of that,
That smooth-faced gentleman, tickling Commodity,
Commodity, the bias of the world,
The world, who of itself is peised well,
Made to run even upon even ground,
Till this advantage, this vile-drawing bias,
This sway of motion, this Commodity,
Makes it take head from all indifferency,
From all direction, purpose, course, intent:
And this same bias, this Commodity,
This bawd, this broker, this all-changing word,
Clapp'd on the outward eye of fickle France,
Hath drawn him from his own determined aid,
From a resolved and honourable war,
To a most base and vile-concluded peace.
And why rail I on this Commodity?
But for because he hath not woo'd me yet:
Not that I have the power to clutch my hand,
When his fair angels would salute my palm;
But for my hand, as unattempted yet,
Like a poor beggar, raileth on the rich.
Well, whiles I am a beggar, I will rail
And say there is no sin but to be rich;
And being rich, my virtue then shall be
To say there is no vice but beggary.
Since Kings break faith upon commodity,
Gain, be my lord, for I will worship thee.

In the last dozen lines of this speech, the syntax is the snip-
snap of sharp distinctions which we have already recognized

from earlier soliloquies as the characteristic utterance of the Bastard's cynical honesty. In the first scene, for instance, we heard:

> For he is but a bastard to the time
> That doth not smack of observation;
> And so am I, whether I smack or no;
> And not alone in habit and device,
> Exterior form, outward accoutrement,
> But from the inward motion to deliver
> Sweet, sweet, sweet poison for the age's tooth:
> Which, though I will not practise to deceive,
> Yet, to avoid deceit, I mean to learn;
> For it shall strew the footsteps of my rising.

The diatribe against Commodity rises suddenly out of what should have been the second member of just such another tart antithesis:

> John, to stop Arthur's title in the whole,
> Hath willingly departed with a part:
> And France, whose armour conscience buckled on, ...

We expect a fourth line to round home pat with a stinging parallel to "willingly departed with a part". Instead, we are made to wait for over a score of lines, while the speaker rings the changes on the theme of expediency. The motive behind this partakes of righteous indignation, but far more of exuberance. The indignation is more than half-assumed, whipped up; we know this not only from the relapse at the end into succinct propositions and distinctions, but also from the way the long sentence, every time it totters like a slowing top, is whipped up again with:

> ... tickling Commodity,
> Commodity, the bias of the world,
> The world, who of itself is peised well, ...

The repetitions—"Commodity, Commodity" and "the world, the world"—are like two lashes of the whip to set the top spinning rapidly once more.

Doubtless similar examples could be found without much difficulty elsewhere in Shakespeare and in other poetic dramatists. Another obvious place to look would be in the poets of the dramatic monologue, such as Browning and Kipling. Yet I think that this kind of poetic syntax is rare, for verse that is in any way dramatic is aimed at the ear, as syntax is not. Besides, so many other devices are available. Pope, for instance, when he puts direct speech in the mouths first of a Baconian scientist, then of a Cartesian, distinguishes one from the other very clearly, but not by syntax, nor by rhythm either, but pre-eminently by rhyme. The couplet, in fact, at least as used by Dryden and by Pope, is capable of rendering only one sort of movement through the mind; it is committed by its very nature to a syntax of antithesis and razor-sharp distinctions. That may be one reason why all the Romantic poets, except Byron, eschewed it.

4. OBJECTIVE SYNTAX

Yet one of the glories of the heroic couplet at its best is the syntactical nicety it permits and even demands. This syntax, however, aspires to and achieves quite different effects from those already considered. I call it *objective*. Poetic syntax is objective when its function is to please us by the fidelity with which it follows a form of action, a movement not through any mind, but in the world at large. This definition is unphilosophical, of course, for any form or movement observed in the external world is, in the process of observation, taken into the poet's mind and must dwell there until it is bodied forth in his writing. Nevertheless, common sense sees an obvious distinction between the movement of a feeling through a man's mind, and the movement of destiny through his life, as through the life of Camillus, the Roman patriot, who was, as Thomas Sackville says,

banisht by them whom he did thus detbind.

It is in relation to this kind of syntax that one can most readily speak, as H. M. McLuhan and Hugh Kenner do, of a sentence

79

as having a plot. Mr. McLuhan has even said that if, according to Fenollosa, every sentence has a plot, then the heroic couplet lends itself to something like "the double-plot of the Elizabethans".

The easiest "plot" to distinguish is the potentially tragic one of "time brings in his revenges":

> And Time that gave doth now his gift confound.

In this Shakespearean line the syntax in unremarkable. There is no tragic reversal on the relative pronoun as in the line from Sackville, or in this, from Cowper, on the poplars felled:

> And the tree is my seat that once lent me a shade . . .

—or in this from Pope:

> The thriving plants ignoble broomsticks made
> Now sweep those Alleys they were born to shade.

Here the relative—"*that* they were born to shade"—must be understood; such omissions are common in Pope, and give not only a conversational tone, but a characteristic syntactical closeness and rapidity, which is delightful and significant in its own right. But this is to anticipate: for the moment, we are concerned with syntactical features not in their own right but according as they mime a pattern of action. Closeness and rapidity of syntax may be virtues in their own right; here we approve them for the vision they convey of human life constantly subject to vicissitudes which appear and develop so suddenly that they are at all times all but uncontrollable. Pope sees human life as a matter of breathless haste and wild energy, whether the patterns he discerns in it are tragic, as above, or heroically affirmative, as when he sums up the Drapier's Letters controversy:

> The Rights a Court attack'd, a Poet sav'd,

—where, again with an omitted relative, he reduces a chapter of history to one clear and rapid narrative line.

It is this above all that marks Blake as a poet of the eighteenth century. In his poems destiny appears as the moral law that works itself out. As Coleridge, in "Dejection", casts analysis and argument into the narrative of a changing mood, so Blake gives to his narratives a syntax as of the proposition, so as to bring out the logic of the moral law that informs his stories and gives them their symbolic meanings:

Pity would be no more
If we did not make somebody Poor;
And Mercy no more could be
If all were as happy as we.

And mutual fear brings peace,
Till the selfish loves increase:
Then Cruelty knits a snare,
And spreads his baits with care.

He sits down with holy fears,
And waters the ground with tears;
Then Humility takes its root
Underneath his foot.

Soon spreads the dismal shade
Of Mystery over his head;
And the Catterpiller and Fly
Feed on the Mystery.

And it bears the fruit of Deceit,
Ruddy and sweet to eat;
And the Raven his nest has made
In its thickest shade.

The Gods of the earth and sea
Sought thro' Nature to find this Tree;
But their search was all in vain:
There grows one in the Human Brain.

In the first stanza of four lines, the effect is very like that of four lines of Pope:

The mind, in Metaphysics at a loss,
May wander in a wilderness of Moss;
The head that turns at super-lunar things,
Pois'd with a tail, may steer on Wilkins' wings.

In reading Pope's lines, as in reading Blake's, the movement of the mind through the first couplet is checked on the rhyme, retracts, and goes through the same motions all over again. The chief difference is that Blake's world is not in such a state of emergency as Pope's is; in Pope's world the mills of God turn much faster. Blake's punctuation is very interesting. Each of his stanzas except the last consists of two complete sentences with a colon or semi-colon between them. This syntactical similarity between the first stanza and those that follow it conveys to us, before we are aware of it, one of the main points Blake wants to make—that each step in his narrative can be reduced to the propositional paradigm or "abstract" framed at the outset. By the same means, Blake slides us into narrative before we are aware of it. The second stanza seems to repeat the syntactical pattern established by the first—a pattern, that is, of two sentences parallel in syntax, rhythm, and meaning. It is only after we have already passed on from the second stanza that we realize that the second sentence of that stanza, while parallel to the first in metre and syntax, is not parallel in meaning, for it has started a narrative upon which we are now fully launched. And that is not the whole story either, for we now perceive that the third sentence is already half-way to narrative, in that, while it repeats the sense of the two sentences in stanza 1, it does not, as they do, put the cart before the horse, looking back from the good things (Pity, Mercy) to the bad things which are the preconditions of their existence, but moves forward in narrative time from the bad thing to the good thing that comes out of it. It is already narrative in that it is putting first things first, not looking back on them, as the opening stanzas did, from the standpoint of "second things", consequences. Pope, in his line about Swift, makes an abstract of one chapter of Irish history, stripping it of all its contingent factors and drawing out of it one simple diagram of forces—the poet saving what the court attacks. Blake does the same, but not for one chapter of human history, rather for the whole of human life—virtues growing from vices. This, I think, is the meaning of his title, "The Human Abstract".

A similar, only less elaborate case is "A Poison Tree":

> I was angry with my friend;
> I told my wrath, my wrath did end.
> I was angry with my foe:
> I told it not, my wrath did grow.
>
> And I water'd it in fears,
> Night and morning with my tears;
> And I sunned it with smiles,
> And with soft deceitful wiles.
>
> And it grew both day and night,
> Till it bore an apple bright;
> And my foe beheld it shine,
> And he knew that it was mine,
>
> And into my garden stole
> When the night had veil'd the pole:
> In the morning glad I see
> My foe outstretch'd beneath the tree.

Mr. H. Coombes, discussing this, remarks: "In a poem of sixteen lines there are some sixteen clauses (not one to each line however), and nearly every line is in a sense self-contained, yet so perfectly does the action 'grow' out of the initial terse but easily natural 'logic' that the poem is a most forcefully coherent whole."[1] It is obvious that one reason why the action grows so easily out of the logic is that, as in "The Human Abstract", each stanza, whether narrative or not, contains two syntactical members, so that every stanza seems to parallel every other one, in syntax as in metre and in rhyme. But the "growth" is easy ("fatally easy", we might say, for the growth of the narrative is also the growth of the dreadful tree) in another way. For in a sense the poem never moves out of the realm of its initial terse logic. The second line of the poem seals off the first; and the fourth, by virtue of the period

[1] H. Coombes, *Literature and Criticism*, p. 95.

after it, appears in just the same way to seal off the third. But in fact it needs the whole of the rest of the poem to lay the demon raised by the third line, as the demon raised in the first was laid in the second. That is, after all, what the poem is about—the delay and the difficulty in exorcizing a passion that is allowed to rankle. Hence the peculiar terse syntax given to the narrative is not just a sleight of hand; it is true to the fact that the implications of the initial "logic" are still being worked out. From this point of view it can be seen that Blake makes great play with the difference between colon and semi-colon. In "A Poison Tree", as in "The Human Abstract", a colon marks the start of the narrative and also the end of it. In "The Human Abstract" the narrative begins after the sixth line and finishes one line from the end. In "A Poison Tree' the narrative begins after the third line and finishes two lines from the end (its conclusion further emphasized by a change to the present tense in the last two lines). It seems that the period, marking off a stage of the narrative inside this frame of colons, is less of a full-stop than the colon is. For Blake, it seems, human life obeyed a rigorous logic, but this logic could only be seen as it worked itself out in the course of life; hence it had to be cast in narrative form. Yet since the course of life was in no way "chancy" or unpredictable, the narrative itself quite properly fell into logical form. Hence his syntax, neither narrative nor propositional, but partaking of both.

It will be remarked that with Blake we are already much nearer than with Pope to the symbolist poem that "*is* what it *says*". We come nearer still, with Keats:

> As when, upon a trancèd summer-night,
> Those green-robed senators of mighty woods,
> Tall oaks, branch-charmèd by the earnest stars,
> Dream, and so dream all night without a stir,
> Save from one gradual solitary gust
> Which comes upon the silence, and dies off,
> As if the ebbing air had but one wave:
> So came these words and went; . . .

84

This falls into the same category as Pope and Blake because the syntax mimes an action outside the mind. The action is seen in smaller compass, that is all—it occupies a few minutes, not a lifetime or many lifetimes or several years. But the mimesis here is of a peculiarly close and vivid kind. The clause which tells of the gust is itself "gradual", for we have to wait for its verb, and the clause which tells of the ebbing air is itself "ebbing air", for the reader is, or feels as if he were, out of breath.

5. SYNTAX LIKE MUSIC

This is much more difficult. And I am not at all happy about drawing a sharp line between Keats's kind of syntax, in the lines just considered, and the syntax that is or aspires to be "like music". But in theory, at any rate, the distinction is sharp enough, if we remember Mrs. Langer's judgment, "what music can actually reflect is only the morphology of feeling", and her remark, "Articulation is its life, but not assertion; expressiveness, not expression." If Mrs. Langer is right, then poetry of this kind (for her there is no other kind) presents human feelings as they are born, develop, gather momentum, branch, sub-divide, coalesce, dwindle, and die away. This of course is just what Coleridge does, in "Dejection", but with this difference—that he there commits himself to defining not only the course of the feeling, but its nature, so that he shall be seen to deal with one feeling, dejection, rather than with others. Now, as Mrs. Langer points out, music does not do this, and all the many attempts to treat it as if it did, by saying this music is sad in such and such a way, this other piece is sad in another way, have come to grief. What sounds sad to one person sounds merry to another. And so Mrs. Langer is forced to say that a sad feeling and a merry feeling may have the same morphology; and that, in music, "The actual function of meaning which calls for permanent contents, is not fulfilled; for the *assignment* of one rather than another possible meaning to each form is never explicitly made." Hence we have to say that poetic syntax is like music when its function is to please us by the fidelity with which it follows a "form of thought" through the poet's mind *but without defining that thought*. (Here our earlier definition of what we mean by "thought" in this context is of the first importance; the "thought", we said, in poetry, is "the experience". Hence it includes, if indeed it is not the same as, Mrs. Langer's "feeling".)

Now in poetry it is not so easy as in music to articulate without asserting; to talk without saying what one is talking about. But, as is well known, this difficulty was circumvented by the use of the objective correlative, the invention of a fable or an "unreal" landscape, or the arrangement of images, not for their own sakes, but to stand as a correlative for the experience that is thus the true subject of a poem in which it is never named. It is true that Mr. Eliot, who put the expression "objective correlative" into currency, speaks as if the function of the correlative is to define, better than by naming, the experience, the feeling, for which it stands. But in the light of Mrs. Langer's distinction, we have to say that it defines the morphology of the feeling, not its distinctive nature. In any case, this convention has healed or blurred the distinction I have used, between "subjective" and "objective" syntax: poems written in this mode employ a syntax that seems to be subjective and objective at once.

What it amounts to can be shown most clearly perhaps by Kenneth Burke's remarks on "The Lost Son", a poem by Theodore Roethke. In the first place, all the poet will say of this poem is that it is "in a sense a stage in a kind of struggle out of the slime; part of a slow spiritual progress, if you will; part of an effort to be born." This fits in with Mrs. Langer's remark about music, that "the actual function of meaning, which calls for permanent contents, is not fulfilled." All the poet offers to give us is the movement through one stage of a struggle, the tensions and resolutions in one part of a progress, the efforts made. To what end they are made, towards what the struggle and the progress are directed—all this can be answered only "in a sense", only "if you will".

Mr. Burke quotes and examines the nine lines of section two of the poem:

> Where do the roots go?
>> Look down under the leaves.
> Who put the moss there?
>> These stones have been here too long.
> Who stunned the dirt into noise?
>> Ask the mole, he knows.
> I feel the slime of a wet nest.
>> Beware Mother Mildew.
> Nibble again, fish nerves.

Mr. Burke comments:

> . . . much is done by a purely Grammatical resource. Thus, the underlying assertion of the first couplet (this mood is like roots, like under-the-leaves) is transformed into a kind of "cosmic" dialogue, split into an interchange between two voices. The next restatement (it is like moss-covered stones) is broken into the same Q-A pattern, but this time the answer is slightly evasive, though still in the indicative ("These stones have been here too long"–a "vatic" way of suggesting that the mood is like stones sunken, and covered heavily). The third couplet (it is like the sound of moles burrowing) is introduced by a slightly longer and more complex question. . . . Also the answer is varied by a shift into the imperative ("Ask the mole").

And he sums up:

> . . . the Grammatical shifts, by dramatizing the sequence of topics, keep one from noting that the stanza is in essence but a series of similarly disposed images (symbolizing what Roethke, in a critical reference, has called "obsessions").[1]

I should prefer to say that the images serve to indicate roughly the area of experience that the poet is dealing with; they limit the number of possible answers to the question, "What is the

---

[1] *Sewanee Review*, Winter 1950, p. 89.

poet talking about?" But a wide range of possible answers remains, and the poem does nothing to narrow this choice any further. Instead it defines, largely by syntactical arrangements and changes, the extent to which the nameless experience is a search, to what extent it is a surrender, to what extent an agony, to what extent a waiting, and so on. As the poet traces the development of the experience, we can see how at one time the element of passive agony, at another the element of active surrender, at another time the waiting, at another time the searching, predominates in the total experience behind the writing. But that experience is never defined, since we are never told to what it surrenders, what it seeks, what it is waiting *for*. Hence this poem seems to me of just the sort that Miss Langer envisages, and the vital part played in it by syntax seems to be, on her showing, "like music".

A subtler case occurs in the first lines of "Gerontion":

> Here I am, an old man in a dry month,
> Being read to by a boy, waiting for rain.
> I was neither at the hot gates
> Nor fought in the warm rain
> Nor knee deep in the salt marsh, heaving a cutlass,
> Bitten by flies, fought.

The repeated "nor" in these lines makes "neither" look rather silly, but that is not my point, which is rather the last word, the repeated "fought". In terms of the prose-sense of this passage, there is no need for this word at all. Its presence certainly gives an interesting twist to an otherwise rather facile rhythm. But I have too much respect for Mr. Eliot to think this his sole reason for tagging on the word. (He has, of course, in his criticism, seemed to deplore such dictation by merely rhythmical considerations.) The word, coming where it does, has the further effect of acting out through syntax the dwindling and the diminution, the guttering frustration and waste, which is the arc of feeling here being presented. The verb, energetic in meaning, and in the active voice, is held up by the three phrases ("knee deep in the salt marsh, heaving a cutlass, bitten by flies"), and this postponing of the issue builds up a tension which the verb would, in the ordinary way, resolve with all the more vigorous *éclat*, in a powerful reverberation. But this it cannot do, having been negated from the first by that "nor" from which it is now so far removed. Hence it has the effect almost of parody, of a shrill and cracked vehemence, like:

> I will do such things,
> What they are yet, I know not, but they shall be
> The terrors of the earth.

Lear's windy threatening is a fine piece of dramatic syntax; Gerontion's is unlike it, because we are not to take him as a person but only a *persona*—he is given a phantasmal life only provisionally, not fully bodied forth. Hence, though this is a tricky case, I regard Eliot's lines as an example of syntax like music.

It is important to realize, however, that, although "objective correlative" and "syntax like music" are principles only recently formulated in poetic theory, both can be found in the poetic practice of poets writing much earlier. Much pre-symbolist verse can be made to toe a symbolist or post-symbolist line.

For instance, this seems to be the place to consider what Hopkins called "the figure of grammar". He found it pre-eminently in Hebrew poetry:

A figure of grammar can be shifted to other words with a change of specific meaning but keeping some general agreement, as of noun over against noun, verb against verb, assertion against assertion, etc., e.g. Foxes (A) have (B) holes (C) and birds of the air (A') have (B—not B' here) nests (C'), or more widely even than this/with a change of words but keeping the grammatical and logical meaning—as/Foxes have holes and birds of the air have nests (that is/Beasts have homes to live in) but the Son of Man has not where to lay His head (that is/Man has not a home to live in): the subjects of the clauses being changed the one does no more than say yes, the other no.

This passage is quoted by Sir Herbert Read in the book I have referred to already. He applies it to the verse of Whitman and of Lawrence, and, by arguing that they are rhetoricians not poets, seems to want to huddle away the Figure of Grammar out of poetry into rhetoric. But even though we agree in calling Whitman a rhetorician in some pejorative sense, it may not be the Figure of Grammar that makes him so. Hopkins, for instance, spoke of Whitman's "rhythm run to seed", and Allen Tate, when he follows Hopkins in this, does so with the specific intention of showing how the Figure of Grammar need not involve this sort of rhythmical decadence. According to Tate it does not do so for St.-John Perse, whose verse is only super-ficially like Whitman's. In Perse's poetry, according to Tate, "the very grammar . . . becomes itself a principle of organiza-tion."[1] And if I understand the critic, this means that Perse's poetry is based upon what Hopkins called the Figure of Gram-mar, and that its syntax is "like music".

For an example of this in English, we can go to Eliot again, to the beginning of "Ash-Wednesday":

1. Because I do not hope to turn again
2. Because I do not hope
3. Because I do not hope to turn
4. Desiring this man's gift and that man's scope
5. I no longer strive to strive towards such things
6. (Why should the aged eagle stretch its wings?)
7. Why should I mourn
8. The vanished power of the usual reign?

9. Because I do not hope to know again
10. The infirm glory of the positive hour
11. Because I do not think
12. Because I know I shall not know
13. The one veritable transitory power
14. Because I cannot drink
15. There, where trees flower, and springs flow, for there is nothing again.

[1] Allen Tate, "Homage to St.-John Perse", *Nine*, No. 3 (1949–50), p. 79.

I have numbered these lines for ease of reference. Now if we compare lines 8, 10, and 13, it will be observed that 10 and 13 are tied together by an end-rhyme, but that 8 and 10 are tied together no less closely by similarity of grammar. What we have here, in fact, is a sort of parity of esteem between rhyme and metre and grammar or syntax. Every line in the second section, except for the last of all, "rhymes" with some one or more lines in the first section. Thus 9 is linked with 8 by end-rhyme, but, as I have remarked, 10 no less "rhymes" with 8 by virtue of grammar. 11 rhymes by syntax with 2. 12 rhymes with 3 by virtue of metre and a certain syntactical similarity, but also by syntax with 5 ("Know I shall not know" echoing "strive to strive"). 13 rhymes through 10 with 8. And 14 rhymes, by metre and syntax, with 2. The two lines left over are 4 and 15, and one could even argue, though this might be straining a little, that these "rhyme" together, simply by virtue of being each the odd one out (though each is linked by end-rhyme with another line in its own section).

This use of syntax as rhyme is certainly nearer to "syntax like music" than to any of the other varieties so far considered. But I confess I am uncertain whether it does not constitute another category again; and to this I now turn.

6 SYNTAX LIKE MATHEMATICS

I make this category on the authority of Valéry, speaking of Mallarmé's interest in syntax:

> In this—and I told him so one day—he approached the attitude of men who in algebra have examined the science of forms and the symbolical part of the art of mathematics. This type of attention makes the structure of expressions more felt and more interesting than their significance or value. Properties of transformations are worthier the mind's attention than what they transform; and I sometimes wonder if a more general notion can exist than the notion of a "proposition" or the consciousness of thinking no matter what.[1]

[1] Variété III, p. 28, quoted Sewell, *The Structure of Poetry*, pp. 151, 152.

In the light of this we have to say that *poetic syntax is like mathematics when its function is to please us in and for itself.*

Now while in practice it may be (indeed it is) very difficult indeed, quite often, to distinguish syntax like music from syntax like mathematics, in theory it is very easy indeed. For the widest possible gulf yawns between this last category and, not only the one before it, but all those so far considered. For all those were alike in appealing for their justification to something outside themselves, which they mimed. All were at bottom *mimetic*, or aspired to be. The syntax of Mallarmé appeals to nothing but itself, to nothing outside the world of the poem.

Hence my hesitation over "Ash-Wednesday"; where the use of syntax as rhyme (if I may be permitted to use once more that extravagant expression) seems to be merely a part of the poem's internal economy, purely a structural device. It may be only that. But I do not think it is. I prefer to think—and after all this is not a sheer act of faith—that when identical syntactical arrangements recur in "Ash Wednesday", they do so not just to knit the poem together, but because the curve of experience presented in the poem has at that point come round upon itself. Hence the syntax of "Ash Wednesday" can, after all, be shepherded into the mimetic fold.

In fact it is hard to find in English any counterpart to Mallarmé from this point of view. I think I have found one however in the "Epistle to a Patron" of that most unjustly neglected contemporary F. T. Prince:

My lord, hearing lately of your opulence in promises and your
                                          house
Busy with parasites, of your hands full of favours, your statutes
Admirable as music and no fear of your arms not prospering, I
                                          have
Considered how to serve you and breed from my talents
These few secrets which I shall make plain
To your intelligent glory. You should understand that I have
                                          plotted

Being in command of all the ordinary engines
Of defence and offence, a hundred and fifteen buildings
Less others less complete: complete, some are courts of serene
                                                    stone
Some the civil structures of a war-like elegance as bridges
Sewers, aqueducts, and citadels of brick with which I declare the
                                                    fact
That your nature is to vanquish. For these I have acquired a
                                                    knowledge
Of the habits of numbers and of various tempers and skill in
                                                    setting
Firm sets of pure bare members which will rise, hanging to-
                                                    gether
Like an argument, with beams, ties and sistering pilasters:
The lintels and windows with mouldings as round as a girl's
                                                    chin; thresholds
To libraries; halls that cannot be entered with a sensation as of
                                                    myrrh
By your vermilion officiers, your sages and dancers. There will
                                                    be chambers
Like the recovery of a sick man, your closet waiting not
Less suitably shadowed than the heart, and the coffers of a ceiling
To reflect your diplomatic taciturnities. . . .

And so this splendid poem goes on. There is no reason why it
should ever stop, for it is plain that under the guise of architect
speaking to patron the poet is speaking to his reader, and
speaking about his poem even as he writes it. For the building
is "like an argument", and the chamber in it "not less suitably
shadowed than the heart". The poem does not even explore
the relationship, actual or ideal, of poet and reader; the poem is
the poem's subject—that is all. And this of course is significant.
For if the structures of expression are to be more interesting
to the reader than the structures of experience behind them,
the only way to induce the right sort of attention in the reader
is to have nothing behind them at all, that is, to have poems
that are meaningless. The only alternative is to have poems that
talk about themselves, as Prince's does.

But this is true only so long as the poet is determined to make his poetry "pure" and "absolute". For in Valéry's formula, it is not necessary that the structure of expressions should be *the only* source of interest in the poem, only that this should be more interesting than anything else. And even Valéry's formula is too narrow. For there is no reason why this sort of syntax, any more than any of the other sorts, should be more than one source of pleasure among many others. It is *poetic* syntax in that it gives poetic pleasure, and it differs from other kinds of syntax only in this—that the pleasure it gives has nothing to do with mimesis. On these terms, any amount of older poetry can be seen to employ syntax-like-mathematics and indeed this category becomes more crowded than any of the others. In particular, the Augustan age sends up one candidate after another:

> Within the couplet the poet worked out as many contrasts and parallels as he could, providing the maximum number of internal geometrical relationships. Denham's lines on the Thames had fascinated later poets with the possibilities of this kind of configuration. They were frequently imitated—too frequently for Swift's pleasure. Their kind of verbal manipulation was improved on, until in Pope a couplet will often suggest a difficult figure in Euclid, its vowels and consonants, its sense-oppositions and sense-attractions, fitted together like arcs and lines.

> "A Fop their Passion, but their Prize a Sot;
> Alive, ridiculous, and dead, forgot!"[1]

The Euclidean reference here is exact. This is a syntax like mathematics, as is Mallarmé's. I have given examples from Pope to illustrate another category of poetic syntax which I have called "objective", and I think there is some danger that the high shine of artifice over the surface of the best Augustan verse will lead readers to think of their syntax as "like mathematics" when in fact it has a more mimetic function, clinging closely to the experience behind it. Still, it cannot be denied

---

[1] *Times Literary Supplement*, Saturday, Jan. 4, 1936.

that it is in the eighteenth century that we find most of this Euclidean syntax.

Yeats may seem to speak of the same thing, though he compares it˙ with mechanics rather than mathematics, when he writes to H. J. C. Grierson in 1912:

> The over childish or over pretty or feminine element in some good Wordsworth and in much poetry up to our date comes from the lack of natural momentum in the syntax. This momentum underlies almost every Elizabethan and Jacobean lyric and is far more important than simplicity of vocabulary. If Wordsworth had found it he could have carried any amount of elaborate English. Byron, unlike the Elizabethans though he always tries for it, constantly allows it to die out in some mind-created construction, but is I think the one great English poet—though one can hardly call him great except in purpose and manhood—who sought it constantly.[1]

But here there is the difficulty of what Yeats means by "natural". He opposes it to "mind-created", which is obviously much the fitter word for the constructions of Denham and Pope. Fenollosa too was much concerned, in his remarks on syntax, for its "momentum"; and if Yeats intended to give to "natural" the full and ambitious sense that Fenollosa gave to it, then his view of syntax would become, in my terms, "objective". This is unlikely, however. In view of Yeats's lifelong preoccupations and of his reference to Wordsworth, it is more probable that he means by "natural" something like "in close touch with living speech". If so, then he esteems momentum in syntax because it assists in the miming of the living speech of those persons (Yeats was quite precise about who they were) who in his view were models of poetic utterance; and in that case, the syntax he asks for is "dramatic".

[1] *Encounter*, No. 2 (Nov. 1953), p. 20.

95

VIII

SYNTAX IN ENGLISH POETRY AND
IN FRENCH

ᴊᴇ

I<small>T</small> is obvious that any attempt to make a hard-and-fast rule about what poetic syntax is or ought to be depends upon an equally stringent rule about poetic language, about what words are or ought to be, in poetry. This is true of both Hulme and Fenollosa, who insist that words in poetry are or ought to be like "things". This is nonsense, of course; yet useful nonsense. Words are not things, nor can any one word be shown to be more of a thing than any other; but the fact remains that in reading poetry we do feel some words or some arrangements of words to partake of the nature of the things they stand for, in a way that other words and arrangements of words do not. All the same, common sense must be allowed to have its say. And common sense forces us to ask why the words of poetry should be thought to be all of one kind. The commonsense position is that words are of different kinds, and that the old-fashioned grammatical classification into "parts of speech" does correspond roughly to the different feelings we have about these different kinds. Hulme and Fenollosa assume that words in poetry are all of one kind; and this assumption rests upon another, that words outside poetry are of only two kinds. They seem to assume that all words are either abstract or concrete, and that by and large concrete words are good for poetry, where abstract words aren't. To be sure they refine on this, since Fenollosa in particular insists that the most abstract words are concrete at bottom, and can be shown to be so in a poetic context. Perhaps they would agree that a word is abstract or concrete not in itself, but only relative to the context in which it occurs. Nevertheless it is not unfair to say that for both of them a word, when it appears, is either abstract or concrete. Is this in fact the case? Must we either pick away at the base of one of Fenollosa's pyramids, or else leap nimbly from one apex to another? Is there no half-way house? And if there is, what is the significance of that for poetry in general and syntax in particular?

In order to answer these questions, it is instructive to look at a foreign language. St.-John Perse reports on his friendship with Gide:

> He told me of the attraction that an exhaustive study of the English language was beginning to exert over him. I, for my part, deplored the denseness of such a concrete language, the excessive richness of its vocabulary and its pleasure in trying to reincarnate the thing itself, as in ideographic writing; whereas French, a more abstract language, which tries to signify rather than represent the meaning, uses words only as fiduciary symbols like coins as values of monetary exchange. English for me was still at the swapping stage.
>
> There was some nodding and shaking of the head. That was precisely, if he was to be believed, just what he most needed at the moment: to take on weight and mass in the language of Newton.[1]

There is no need to point out that Perse favours a view of language quite at odds with what Hulme and Fenollosa and Pound, in their different ways and with varying degrees of sophistication, have urged upon the English poet and his readers.

This too, like all theories of syntax, turns out to rest upon a philosophy, an inclusive attitude towards human life and human knowledge:

[1] St.-J. Perse, "André Gide: 1909", tr. Mina Curtiss, *Sewanee Review*, LX, 4, p. 601.

French literature, born in a civilization of courts, of salons, cliques, and of philosophers' garrets, and thus eminently social, anti-metaphysical and anti-poetic, is rediscovering its infinite in the very depths of the well of the human heart, as unfathomable as any other for the Frenchman, who is by nature an analyst and a psychologist. English literature sprang from a more material civilization and, more enamoured of nature, is rediscovering its infinite in the cosmic abyss![1]

This too fits in very well with much we have observed already. Mr. Kenner, as a champion of "ideographic writing", sneers at "the Cartesian thinkers' hatred of things outside themselves"; this may serve as a gloss on what is meant here by "psychologist". Similarly, if the Frenchman is "by nature an analyst", he will obviously find himself on the other side of the fence from Hulme, for whom analysis is only a form of the "extensive manifold" with which, he says, poetry has nothing to do— "The intellect always analyses—when there is a synthesis it is baffled. That is why the artist's work seems mysterious."

This is a view of poetry at the opposite extreme from Mr. Kenner's:

> Looking about the world, we know *things*. On a page of poetry there are set in motion the intelligible species of *things*. Words are solid, they are not ghosts or pointers. The poet connects, arranges, defines, *things*: pearls and eyes; garlic, sapphires and mud.[2]

On this showing to speak of words as "fiduciary symbols" is to make of them ghosts or pointers.

§ 2

Of course, to speak of the nature of French language, the nature of English, is hopelessly unscientific. But the contrast between French and English on this point is useful and suggestive. Dryden, for instance, indebted as he was to French models in Corneille, Boileau, St. Evremond, compared French with

[1] St.-J. Perse, "Andre Gide: 1909", tr. Mina Curtiss, *op cit.*, p. 600.
[2] *The Poetry of Ezra Pound*, p. 77.

English in just the same terms; the language of the French, he said, "is not strung with sinews like our English; it has the nimbleness of a greyhound, but not the bulk and body of a mastiff." Dryden's "bulk and body" corresponds to the French writer's apprehension of "weight and mass". The Earl of Roscommon, Dryden's contemporary, made the comparison thus:

> But who did ever in French authors see
> The comprehensive English Energy?
> The weighty Bullion of one Sterling Line,
> Drawn to French Wire, would thro' whole Pages shine.

And this brings us closer to Fenollosa, for whom "weightiness" and "energy" go together; the weight and mass do not or need not make the verse inert, quite the contrary. On the other hand, it may make it short-winded: Roscommon's contrast between the "one Sterling Line" and the "whole pages" corresponds perhaps to Fenollosa's vindication of only the briefest and simplest of syntactical forms. But this is to read too much into one slender clue.

Hofmannsthal remarks, in the *Book of Friends*, "French prose at its highest level is more sensual in the intellectual field and in the sensual more intellectual than the German at its present level." And again, "One advantage of the French language is that it can form spontaneously the plural of sensual *abstracta: les fatigues, les vides, les noirs.*"[1] This last is obviously an example of how French is "sensual in the intellectual field". English can form such plurals—"leaden-eyed despairs", "to suffer woes which Hope thinks infinite". I have not seen it remarked how English Romantic poets, disliking the personifications of the Augustans, evaded them by merely tacking an "—s" on the end. This could be taken as an amusing revelation of their hypocrisy. But that would be wrong. The addition of the "—s" makes a world of difference. When abstractions appear in the plural they are no longer to the same degree abstractions. When an eighteenth-century poet writes "Woe", "Despair", we are restive, feeling how many different human

[1] *Selected Prose*, tr. Mary Hottinger and Tania and James Stern, pp. 371, 373.

experiences have been "stunned", deprived of all their painful immediacy and uniqueness, in order to come under the one abstracted term. With Keats's "despairs" and Shelley's "woes", we do not feel this. The poet, by using the plural, acknowledges that there are many kinds of despair, many kinds of woe; if he does not choose to dwell on them now, it is not that he does not know of them—he asks us to let the word serve for the moment, as we read. What we have in fact is a word that is neither abstraction nor concretion, but something in between. And this may be what our French authority means by "fiduciary symbols". If Hofmannsthal is right in saying that French sensualizes the intellectual and intellectualizes the sensual, he may be saying that the tendency of the language is towards words as symbols *in this sense.* Concretions are milked of their concreteness, abstractions are flushed with sense, until both sorts of word can live together on a common symbolic level. Perhaps this corresponds to our intuition of what happens as we read a passage of French.

This is the most important point I want to make, and I want to develop it. But first this is the place perhaps to dispose of a possible confusion. The passages I have quoted come from some fugitive recollections by a French poet, St.-John Perse, of a French novelist André Gide. Now it is a fact that the movement in English poetry that drew upon the authorities of T. E. Hulme and Ernest Fenollosa was also characterized by appeals to French prose as a model. Ezra Pound is the case in point:

> . . . no man can now write really good verse unless he knows Stendhal and Flaubert.

This appears to make against our case that the tendency of French, at least of French prose, is away from the "ideographic writing" that Pound has developed in his verse. But the point can be cleared up if I appeal, yet once more, to Hugh Kenner:

> What Flaubert actually did was arrange not primarily words but things; or words as *mimesis* of things. Out of an odour, a

waft of talk, a plume of smoke, the flare of gaslight, the disposition, relative to the carpet and windows, of certain furniture in a certain room, the world of Frederic Moreau emerges with palpable and autonomous immediacy. The significant action of the novel, in contradistinction to the diagrammable "plot", obstructed by dull descriptions, that emerges from a poor translation, consists in the interactions of, the tensions set up between, these items. That is the meaning of *le mot juste.*[1]

This is clearly a response to Flaubert very different from Proust's, when he observes, "The conjunction '*et*' has nowhere in Flaubert's works the purpose assigned to it by grammar. It marks a pause in a rhythmical measure and divides a picture", or, "That whole second page of *L'Éducation sentimentale* is made of imperfects, except when a change intervenes, an action of which the protagonists generally are things."[2] Proust seems more interested in the exact nature of the tensions and interactions than in the things thus related. Pound too is interested in these relations, yet he does not use syntax to present them, but rhythm instead. It may be objected of course that this is just the difference between prose and verse; in which case one goes on to argue that authentic syntax has no place in poetry. At any rate, this shows how it could come about that a master of French prose syntax was adopted as a model by English poets who were destroying syntax nearly altogether.

§ 3

St.-John Perse wants words to be "fiduciary symbols". "Fiduciary", says the dictionary, "held or given in trust; relating to a trustee." What is in question plainly is a sort of contract entered into tacitly by speaker and hearer, writer and reader; a convention which both observe. This would be anathema to Fenollosa, for whom the only contract the poet

---

[1] *The Poetry of Ezra Pound*, p. 256.
[2] Quoted in the Introduction to *Essays on Language and Literature*, ed. J. L. Hevesi.

should honour is that between himself and "nature". Hulme goes further and says that the contracts normally in being between speaker and hearer are only a hindrance to the poet. Hence, critics who follow Hulme's lead (and that is to say, most of the critics influential today) lay great stress upon the poet's task in breaking down the reader's "stock responses", getting through or behind the existent conventions, flouting the established contract in order to enter into another. By this course of reasoning, one arrives at the notion that in order to become a reader of poetry the individual must go through a period of strenuous training and rehabilitation. St.-John Perse envisages another possibility, that of the poet communicating with his readers in terms of contracts to which the reader is accustomed. As all readers are most accustomed to various sorts of prose, it seems likely that on this view poetry and prose will differ only in degree, where to proponents of the other argument they will differ in kind.

What is the nature of the contract that obtains between the poet and his reader? Or rather (since the whole idea of "contract" is now being challenged), what has been the nature of such poetic contracts in the past? One obvious clue is the idea of "genre": the poet, by advertising that his poem is to be elegy or epistle or satire or epic, asks of his reader a certain kind of attention and promises him in return a certain kind of profit. This advertisement may appear even in a title, or else it can emerge from certain easily recognized features of the verse as soon as the reading begins; such are metrical forms, for instance, traditionally connected with one genre rather than another, such as the elegiac stanza; or they can take the form of a certain pitch of tone (epic diction is "lofty"); or there are such features as the epic simile. C. S. Lewis, when he defends Milton against Dr. Leavis, says in effect that when Dr. Leavis reads *Paradise Lost*, he refuses to honour the contract proper to the heroic poem; he gives the wrong sort of attention and expects the wrong sort of profit. On the other hand Dr. Leavis can retort that ultimately every poem is unique, and therefore every poem requires a contract valid only for itself. Every poem, even within the convention of its genre, establishes its own convention; and he can argue that when he says Milton asks too much of his readers, he means that he asks more than even other epic poets have asked for. The contract involved in *Paradise Lost* (he may say) is an unacceptable one, quite unjustly weighted in favour of the poet and against the reader. The poet asks too much and gives too little in return.

But the contract we speak of here is one that is common to the reading of poetry in general, to each and every poem, anterior to the more specific contracts of genre. It concerns something that the reader must grant to the poet before he begins to read any poetry at all. At least one provision of that contract rests upon the nature of reading as an activity taking time:

> The nature of any particular semantic reaction, or any part of a total semantic reaction, is conditional on what precedes and follows it. As all speech signs are presented in a certain time-order, this is a very important point.[1]

In the less rebarbative language of criticism this means no more than the well-worn truth that any word is defined by its context. But it has the advantage of emphasizing that this is not peculiar to those arrangements of language traditionally known as "literature". It is a feature of all forms of linguistic communication:

> It is almost comic to note the difficulty with which we are confronted when we try to establish the *precise* meaning of a word which, in the ordinary routine of life, we use daily to our complete satisfaction. Take, for instance, the word Time. Caught on the wing, it is perfectly lucid, defined and honest. It fulfils its purpose faithfully, so long as that purpose is to form part of a conventional statement, so long as he who employs it has something definite to say. But isolate it, clip its wings, and it turns and takes its revenge. ... It is something entirely different from what it

---

[1] Pollock, *The Nature of Literature*, pp. 42, 43.

was, an enigma, an abyss, a source of mental torment. The same is true of the word Life, and of many other words.[1]

This, then, is one of the provisions in the contract between poet and reader. The reader undertakes not to tear a word from its context and scrutinize it in isolation. The poet reserves the right to use at any point a word that may seem, by its appearance, to have little or no meaning; he engages, in return, to give it meaning in the context of the whole. This, as we saw, is the contract implicit in Keats's "leaden-eyed despairs".

None of this is very startling or novel, until we pause to ask what is meant by "context". What is the contextual unit? If we say that by "in its context" the poet means "in the context of the whole poem", then we are faced with Ezra Pound's *Cantos*, a poem of enormous length, which has appeared in snatches during the past twenty-five years and is still incomplete. If we are baffled by the significance of any word that has appeared in the sections so far published, we can be told to wait until we see it in the context of the whole poem.

For the ideographic writers who seem in other respects contemptuous of the whole idea of the contract ("You need grant me nothing", they seem to say. "The thing is there on the page, embodied; the process is there, enacted"), turn out to insist rigorously on the form of contract that insists on reading in context—"everything will fall into place in the context of the whole." How does this reading of the contract differ from Valéry's?

Chiefly, in this: that Valéry's poet gives us the articulation as he goes along, but asks us to wait till the end for the meaning of the things articulated; Pound is a poet who gives the "things" as they go along, but asks us to wait till the end before we see the connection between them. This is clear from Valéry's insistence that "Time" is manageable enough, so long as we take it as "part of a conventional statement". It becomes unmanageable only when we take it "apart from its neighbours . . . in

---

[1] Valéry in *Essays on Language and Literature*, ed. Hevesi, pp. 73, 74.

isolation from its momentary function". It is when we take the words in isolation, that they become, as they became for Lord Chandos, "congealed into eyes which stared at me and into which I was forced to stare back—whirlpools which gave me vertigo and, reeling incessantly, led into the void." Pound can retort that he never takes a word "apart from its neighbours"; on the contrary, to give a word three or four selected neighbours is the clue to the ideographic method. On the other hand, it certainly cannot then be said "to form part of a conventional statement". Valéry's poetry can plainly find room for at least the forms of conventional syntax, where Pound's cannot.

IX

SYNTAX IN THE BLANK-VERSE OF WORDSWORTH'S *PRELUDE*

ﾃﾟ

WE have to understand that when St.-John Perse speaks of the Englishman as enamoured of "nature", he means the "nature" of Isaac Newton. If the clue to Newton had not been given, we might have gone astray. We might have thought first of Wordsworth. For it is Wordsworth who springs most readily to mind as the sort of English poet that the Frenchman finds alien, the poet "enamoured of nature" and "rediscovering (his) infinite in the cosmic abyss". But the abyss, we now realize, is not what evoked in Wordsworth "fleeting moods of shadowy exultation"; what the French poet means is "a world of atoms in motion, devoid of all secondary sense qualities, such as colour, scent, taste and sound, ordered by causal laws and explicable only in terms of mathematics"[1]—in short, the world of abstract "matter" in which the early experimenters seemed to find themselves, when they followed out the implications of their conscientiously "concrete" experiments.

Far from making against Wordsworth, Perse's view of poetic language, I shall suggest, is the one best fitted to account for some of Wordsworth's verse. Only in terms of words as "fiduciary symbols" can Wordsworth's blank-verse in *The*

[1] R. L. Brett, *The Third Earl of Shaftesbury: A Study in Eighteenth-century Literary Theory*, p. 14.

106

Prelude be properly appreciated. In those passages of *The Prelude* where Wordsworth is trying to convey most exactly the effect of the natural world upon himself, his words ("ties" and "bonds" and "influences" and "powers") will carry the reader only (as Valéry says) so long as he does not loiter, so long as they are taken, as coins are taken, "as values of monetary exchange". Wordsworth's words have meaning so long as we trust them. They have just such meaning, and just as much meaning, as Perse and Valéry suggest.

We can make a start by pointing out that Wordsworth's world is not pre-eminently a world of "things". His language has not, in St.-John Perse's sense, "weight and mass". It is not concrete. Because in the Preface to *Lyrical Ballads* Wordsworth castigated some earlier poets for giving no proof that they had ever truly *looked* at natural phenomena, it is often supposed that his own verse is full of such phenomena rendered in all their quiddity and concreteness. But this is a sort of optical illusion. What Wordsworth renders is not the natural world but (with masterly fidelity) the effect that world has upon him. He is at all points a very long way from "trying to reincarnate the thing itself, as in ideographic writing". As Lionel Trilling remarks:

> Wordsworth never did have the special and perhaps modern sensibility of his sister or of Coleridge, who were so aware of exquisite particularities. His finest passages are moral, emotional, subjective; whatever visual intensity they have comes from his response to the object, not from his close observation of it.[1]

On the contrary, I have heard more than one student complain of Wordsworth's diction that it is too "abstract". I shall argue that the diction of *The Prelude* is neither abstract nor concrete, but something between the two.

This gives me the chance to introduce a very weighty objection to Ernest Fenollosa's theory of poetic language. It will be remembered that according to him, "At the base of the pyramid

[1] Lionel Trilling, *The Liberal Imagination*, p. 133.

lie *things*, but stunned, as it were." T. C. Pollock, however, sees in this view the fallacy of "Misplaced Concreteness":

> If an abstract term is the sign of an abstraction from an individual experience (E) or a group of individual experiences (E), a non-abstract or a concrete term would be the sign of that from which the abstraction was drawn, the non-abstract individual experience (E) or the non-abstract individual experiences (E) in the group of experiences (E). The opposite of an abstract term would therefore be, not the name of a specific or "concrete" object, but the sign of a total or concrete *experience* (E). The error arises because of the assumption that the abstraction is from *objects*, instead of from *experiences* (E). (On the contrary, what we call "objects" are psychologically abstractions from *experiences* (E).)

As Pollock goes on to show,[1] this statement is only the counterpart in linguistic theory of a fact of linguistic history, the fact established by Jespersen that originally words stood for whole *experiences*, which were only subsequently broken down into "seen" things and "unseen" feelings about them, or significances in them. Fenollosa's account of metaphor is at odds with Jespersen, as his account of abstraction is at odds with Pollock.

Now if Wordsworth was concerned to render his responses to the natural world, he was concerned with experiences, and these were "concretions" from which he did not care to abstract (as his sister and Coleridge did) that part of them which we call "objects" or "things". It follows that ideographic writing, in which words embody things, is *more abstract than* writing in which words are fiduciary symbols for elements of an experience.

This view of words as symbols is advanced by Coleridge in a famous passage from *Biographia Literaria*:

> The best part of human language, properly so called, is derived from reflection on the acts of the mind itself. It is formed by a voluntary appropriation of fixed symbols to internal acts, to

---

[1] Pollock, *The Nature of Literature*, p. 62.

processes and results of imagination, the greater part of which have no place in the consciousness of uneducated man; though in civilized society, by imitation and passive remembrance of what they hear from their religious instructors and other superiors, the most uneducated share in the harvest which they neither sowed nor reaped.

It will be recalled that this statement is made when Coleridge is objecting to Wordsworth's recommendation of rustic language, on the grounds that such language can provide only poor and meagre syntax:

> The rustic, from the more imperfect development of his faculties, and from the lower state of their cultivation, aims almost solely to convey insulated facts, either those of his scanty experience or his traditional belief; while the educated man chiefly seeks to discover and express those connections of things, or those relative bearings of fact to fact, from which some more or less general law is deducible. For facts are valuable to a wise man, chiefly as they lead to the discovery of the indwelling law, which is the true being of things, the sole solution of their modes of existence, and in the knowledge of which consists our dignity and our power.

Coleridge points out, what Perse and Valéry have led us to expect, that if a language is deficient in "fixed symbols" for "internal acts", it will also be deficient in syntax. I shall proceed to show that Wordsworth, when he abandoned rustic diction and took to rendering "internal acts", "processes and results of imagination", used for the purpose an elaborate syntax, and that an important part of his vocabulary is neither abstract nor concrete, but made up of fixed fiduciary symbols.

In *The Prelude* the syntax is elaborately correct:

> I deem not profitless these fleeting moods
> Of shadowy exultation: not for this,
> That they are kindred to our purer mind
> And intellectual life; but that the soul,
> Remembering how she felt, but what she felt
> Remembering not, retains an obscure sense

> Of possible sublimity, to which
> With growing faculties she doth aspire,
> With faculties still growing, feeling still
> That whatsoever point they gain, they still
> Have something to pursue.

Dr. Leavis comments on this passage:

> It would be difficult to suggest anything more elusive than
> this possibility which the soul glimpses in "visionary" moments
> and,
>
> > "Remembering how she felt, but what she felt
> > Remembering not,"
>
> retains an "obscure sense" of. Perhaps it will be agreed that,
> though Wordsworth no doubt was right in feeling that he had
> something to pursue, the critic here is in a different case. If these
> "moments" have any significance for the critic (whose business
> it is to define the significance of Wordsworth's poetry), it will
> be established, not by dwelling upon or in them, in the hope of
> exploring something that lies hidden in or behind their vague-
> ness, but by holding firmly on to that sober verse in which they
> are presented.[1]

I may be misreading Dr. Leavis, but it seems to me that what
is recommended here is what Perse and Valéry recommend:
taking the verse at a run, not pausing on the nouns for fear they
congeal into the staring unfathomable eyes that appalled
Hofmannsthal, but attending rather to the syntactical weave. If
this is what Dr. Leavis means, the testimony is all the more
valuable as coming from a reader who in other cases (on Milton,
for instance, as we have seen) is cautious not to grant the poet
all that he asks for. What Wordsworth asks for here is for all
his words to be considered only in their context. Yet it is
different from what Pound asks for in the *Cantos*. These moods,
exultations, senses, sublimities, and faculties will be no clearer
at the end of *The Prelude* than they are here; and yet the poem
will not be a botch, for what will be clear at the end is the
relationship between them, the articulation. The nouns are not

---

[1] F. R. Leavis, *Revaluation*, pp. 173, 174.

concrete; but the verbs are, and may be lingered over. In short, this is poetry where the syntax counts enormously, counts for nearly everything.

Earlier, however, in his chapter on Wordsworth, Dr. Leavis has remarked of this blank-verse:

> Wordsworth in such passages as are in question produces the mood, feeling or experience and at the same time appears to be giving an explanation of it. The expository effect sorts well with —blends into—the characteristic meditative gravity of the emotional presentment ("emotion recollected in tranquillity"), and in the key passages, where significance seems specially to reside, the convincing success of the poetry covers the argument: it is only by the most resolute and sustained effort (once it occurs to one that effort is needed) that one can pay to the argument, as such, the attention it appears to have invited and satisfied.[1]

And Dr. Leavis directs us to William Empson to see how ill the argument stands up to scrutiny, once one gives attention to it.

On this showing, the syntax of *The Prelude* is not doing what it offers to do. It seems to be explaining, while in fact it is meditating, ruminating, at all events *experiencing* more fully than one does when one explains. But I am not sure that Wordsworth even pretends to explain. Elsewhere Dr. Leavis makes the point like this:

> Even if there were not so much poetry to hold the mind in a subtly incompatible mode of attention, it would still be difficult to continue attending to the philosophic argument, because of the way in which the verse, evenly meditative in tone and movement, goes on and on, without dialectical suspense and crisis or rise and fall. By an innocently insidious trick Wordsworth, in this calm ruminative progression, will appear to be pre-occupied with a scrupulous nicety of statement, with a judicial weighing of alternative possibilities, while actually making it more difficult to check the argument from which he will emerge, as it were inevitably, with a far from inevitable conclusion.[2]

[1] F. R. Leavis, *op cit.*, p. 159.
[2] *Ibid.*, p. 162.

Here the expression, "an innocently insidious trick", sends us back to the idea of Wordsworth's syntax as somehow conjuror's patter. On the other hand the "movement" that "goes on and on without dialectical suspense and crisis or rise and fall" is, it seems, one of the elements that work against argument. And this movement (this is my point) is as much a movement of syntax, a movement of the mind, as it is a movement in the ear. "Dialectical" admits as much. The syntax therefore presents what is really going on, meditation, not argument; and it is therefore authentic, not a play of misleading forms. This confirms me in my original explanation: that this is largely a poetry of verbal symbols which must be taken on trust (almost but not quite like notes or chords in music), for the sake of the articulations jointed between them.

§ 3

Mr. Empson and Dr. Leavis, I suggest, were wrong to think that this poetry aimed at even the effect of philosophic argument. That Wordsworth thought, at Coleridge's instigation, that he might be a philosophic poet is here beside the point; we are speaking of what the poetry does, not of what the poet intended it to do. And in any case, this is the prelude to a philosophic poem, not the poem itself. When that poem appeared, the poetry was not of this kind, as Dr. Leavis acknowledges—"the doctrinal passages of *The Excursion* . . . are plain enough."

The critics were misled, not by the syntax of *The Prelude*, but by its vocabulary, which appears to be "abstract". It is certainly more "abstract" than a great deal of English poetry, but as I have argued, it is not abstract in any strict sense. Its verbs are concrete, and its nouns are verbal symbols, neither concrete nor abstract. That it was the vocabulary that got in Dr. Leavis's way is proved, I think, by his admission that, for him, the Hartleian poem of 1805–6 gives more the effect of philosophic argument than the revised version of 1850. Dr.

Leavis presents what he calls "a representative improvement", by printing a passage in both the versions. At the risk of being tedious, I shall present both passages, and consider Dr. Leavis's comments on them. First, the version of 1805–6 (lines 238–266):

> Bless'd the infant Babe,
> (For with my best conjectures I would trace
> The progress of our Being) blest the Babe,
> Nurs'd in his Mother's arms, the Babe who sleeps
> Upon his Mother's breast, who, when his soul
> Claims manifest kindred with an earthly soul,
> Doth gather passion from his Mother's eye!
> Such feelings pass into his torpid life
> Like an awakening breeze, and hence his mind
> Even [in the first trial of its powers]
> Is prompt and watchful, eager to combine
> In one appearance, all the elements
> And parts of the same object, else detach'd
> And loth to coalesce. Thus day by day,
> Subjected to the discipline of love,
> His organs and recipient faculties
> Are quicken'd, are more vigorous, his mind spreads,
> Tenacious of the forms which it receives.
> In one beloved presence, nay and more
> In that most apprehensive habitude
> And those sensations which have been deriv'd
> From this beloved Presence, there exists
> A virtue which irradiates and exalts
> All objects through all intercourse of sense.
> No outcast he, bewilder'd and depress'd:
> Along his infant veins are interfus'd
> The gravitation and the filial bond
> Of nature, that connect him with the world.
> Emphatically such a Being lives,
> An inmate of this *active* universe.

In 1850 this becomes (lines 233–254):

> Blest the infant Babe,
> (For with my best conjecture I would trace

> Our Being's earthly progress) blest the Babe,
> Nursed in his Mother's arms, who sinks to sleep
> Rocked on his Mother's breast; who with his soul
> Drinks in the feelings of his Mother's eye!
> For him, in one dear Presence, there exists
> A virtue which irradiates and exalts
> Objects through widest intercourse of sense.
> No outcast he, bewildered and depressed:
> Along his infant veins are interfused
> The gravitation and the filial bond
> Of nature that connect him with the world.
> Is there a flower, to which he points with hand
> Too weak to gather it, already love
> Drawn from love's purest earthly fount for him
> Hath beautified that flower; already shades
> Of pity cast from inward tenderness
> Do fall around him upon aught that bears
> Unsightly marks of violence or harm.
> Emphatically such a Being lives
> Frail creature as he is, helpless as frail,
> An inmate of this active universe . . .

Dr. Leavis remarks, "No one is likely to dispute that the later version is decidedly the more satisfactory." However, I mean to dispute it.

I prefer the earlier version in the first place because it does more to deserve that "active" which in 1805 got italics denied to it in 1850. Not only are there more active verbs in the first version, but they are more energetic. In 1805 the child *claims* kindred and *gathers* passion, where in 1850 he "drinks in" feeling. His mind *spreads*, is eager to combine, tenacious and *apprehensive*. (The Latinate pun delivers the muscular grasp of the policeman apprehending the lag.) The later version is mawkish, emphasizing the frailty of the child, his weakness. In the first version the Mother's love is an energy, comparable with the force of gravitation and the chemical force that stirs the torpid life. ("Torpid", of course, was a technical term of eighteenth-century science.) In the later version, the Mother's love is presented as tenderness, and even then as combined or confused with pity. The "gravitation", which survives into the later version, is out of place there, in a context of imagery that is predominantly and weakly visual ("*shades* of pity"), where at first it had been muscular and dynamic. The pseudo-syntax of the rhetorical question ("Is there a flower . . .?") goes along with this pervasive slackening of tension, this retarded and unsteadied movement.

If I ask myself what grounds Dr. Leavis can have for preferring the later version, I can only suppose he is attracted by the relative concreteness (heaven knows it is phantasmal enough) of the flower and even the "Unsightly marks of violence or harm". I would sum up the difference between these two versions by saying that, in the earlier draft, Wordsworth is rendering the experience of being a child at the mother's breast. He is doing this in the only way possible, from inside the child's mind, by rendering in his verse the movements of the child's consciousness, stirring here, checked or sluggish there, drawn this way by powerful currents, dammed back somewhere else. In the later version the poet is sometimes inside the child's mind, sometimes inside the mother's, sometimes inside the spectator's; and by thus shifting his point of view, he denies himself the chance of rendering with fidelity the movements in the child's mind or the mother's or the spectator's. Undoubtedly the language of the earlier version appears more abstract, but it is not therefore ratiocinative. It seems to me that its strength is all in its energetic verbs, and the nouns that attend them ("powers", "elements", "parts", "forms", "sensations", "objects") are correspondingly thin and general. And of course this energy in representing movements of the mind fits in with the fact that Hartley, Wordsworth's master here, was the last of the mechanic psychologists such as influenced Pope, who explained the movements of the mind in terms drawn ultimately from mechanics.

Mr. John Jones, in his very valuable book on Wordsworth,[1] has lately insisted on the extent to which Wordsworth always thought in these eighteenth-century terms:

> There is ... a conservatism in the context of Wordsworth's thought. He is not in revolt against the Great Machine, the master-image of eighteenth-century science and philosophy. Only the phrase is unwordsworthian (though there is enough of pure eighteenth-century poetic in him to allow a reference to his wife's spirit, in relation to her body, as "the very pulse of the machine"): he would prefer something more supple, like "this universal frame of things". His complaint is that nobody has as yet observed its component parts with sufficiently devoted care, or experienced fully the power and beauty of its movement.
>
> In *The Prelude*, Wordsworth uses the word "things" with astonishing frequency. The Concordance reveals that the 1850 text alone accounts for about one-third of its occurrences in the entire bulk of his poetry. "I looked for universal things"; "I conversed with things that really are"; Wordsworth will make his verse "deal boldly with substantial things"—the word is clearly and consistently referred to the main theme of the poem. His search for universal things is on one side a search for particularity: in his insistence upon constancy, boundedness, irreducibility, he betrays the imaginative impression of a traditional English materialism. But he is more than a materialist, in that he enquires not only for the particular but for the powerful. Here his resources are heavily taxed. In order to express essential energy, he is too often led to personify spirit, motion, power itself, in a context of vague declamation. ...

But Wordsworth can do better than that. In passages such as the one just considered, of 1805, he conveys the power as well as the particularity, the different kinds of pulse in the natural machine, by the precisely discriminated energies of his verbs, which concretely act out the powers he is speaking of. In him perhaps one may applaud what Fenollosa applauded in Shakespeare, his "persistent, natural, and magnificent use of hundreds of transitive verbs".

[1] John Jones, *The Egotistical Sublime: A History of Wordsworth's Imagination*, pp. 34, 35.

X

BERKELEY AND YEATS: SYNTAX AND METRE

༄ঌঌঌঌঌঌঌঌঌঌঌঌঌঌঌঌঌঌঌঌঌঌঌঌঌ

Hugh Kenner, writing of the damage done to poetry by Descartes and Locke, comments as follows:

> When the mind no longer lays hold of things, when it does no more than construct its own world according to the hints afforded by sensation, when it knows nothing but its own "ideas", poetic modes of statement, which work by the juxtaposition of objects, are immediately relegated to the status of day-dream . . . The poem affords nothing real.[1]

It is easy, indeed it is normal, to connect Berkeley with the movement in philosophy that Mr. Kenner objects to. Berkeley, it is usually supposed, pressed one stage further the process started in England by Locke, away from "things" towards "ideas". (It is important, of course, to keep the quotation-marks round "ideas", as Mr. Kenner does; by "ideas" Berkeley means "sense-impressions"—the "thing" is only the origin of the impression, the impression itself is something else, an "idea".) Locke, we say, moved the so-called secondary qualities out of apparently "external" reality into the mind; colour, for instance, became a function of the optic nerves. Berkeley points out that, having done so much, Locke might as well do

---

[1] *The Poetry of Ezra Pound*, pp. 95, 96.

the rest and move into the mind the so-called primary qualities also, such as extension. Hence Berkeley takes his place in the line of succession from Locke to Hume, and becomes the father of European idealism.

All this is perfectly true. That the idealists learnt from Berkeley is a matter of fact. But in arguing like this we confuse Berkeley's strategy with his ultimate objective. If the mind is a bag into which Locke put a lot of apparently external "things", then Berkeley gathers up the things that Locke left outside and pops them in also. But this is to halt midway. Having got everything into the bag, he puts his fist to the bottom; the bag turns inside out and there everything is, outside the bag again, once more an external reality.

This is not offered as an argument, only as the statement of a position. The case has been argued elsewhere.

In any case we have found difficulties in the way of accepting Hugh Kenner's generalization, based on Fenollosa, that "poetic modes of statement . . . work by the juxtaposition of objects." It turned out that Wordsworth's blank-verse, for instance, did not work in this way. It may be therefore that Berkeley's view of language can be shown to be more sympathetic to the poet than Mr. Kenner would lead us to think. And it is as a philosopher of language that I shall consider him.

Berkeley invites this sort of attention. He is generally acknowledged to be a master of English prose, and it would be odd if so able a practitioner should be unacceptable as a theorist. In fact, as he hints very broadly himself, some of his central arguments could with profit be put into linguistic terms. His criticism of Locke's "material substance", for instance, would then appear to be a recognition by Berkeley of a submerged metaphor (the table that "stands under" the knives and forks) coming covertly to life in the middle of Locke's argument. But this again is not my business here. I aim only to put together a number of observations by Berkeley on the nature of language, and to see what they imply as regards the nature and the function of syntax in poetry.

We may observe, to begin with, that Berkeley is as fierce an enemy of "abstraction" as Hulme or Fenollosa:

For example, the mind having observ'd that *Peter, James* and *John*, etc. resemble each other, in certain common agreements of shape and other qualities, leaves out of the complex or compounded idea it has of *Peter, James*, etc. that which is peculiar to each, retaining only what is common to all; and so makes an abstract idea wherein all the particulars equally partake, abstracting intirely from and cutting off all those circumstances and differences, which might determine it to any particular existence. And after this manner it is said we come by the abstract idea of *man* or, if you please, humanity or humane nature, wherein 'tis true, there's included colour, because there is no man but has some colour, but then it can be neither white, nor black, nor any particular colour; because there is no one particular colour wherein all men partake. So likewise there is included stature, but then 'tis neither tall stature, nor low stature, nor yet middle stature, but something abstracted from all these; and so of the rest. . . .

Whether others have this wonderful faculty of *abstracting their ideas*, they best can tell: for my self I dare be confident I have it not. I have indeed a faculty of imagining, or representing to my self the ideas of those particular things I have perceiv'd and of variously compounding and dividing them. I can imagine a man with two heads or the upper parts of a man joyn'd to the body of a horse. I can consider the hand, the eye, the nose each by itself abstracted or separated from the rest of the body. But then whatever hand or eye I imagine, it must have some particular shape or colour. Likewise the idea of man that I frame to my self, must be either of a white, or a black, or a tawny, a streight, or a crooked, a tall or a low, or a middle-sized man. I cannot by any effort of thought conceive the abstract idea above described. And it is equally impossible for me to form the abstract idea of motion distinct from the body moving, and which is neither swift nor slow, curvilinear nor rectilinear; and the like may be said of all other abstract general ideas whatsoever.

We can compare with this Fenollosa's example, with which Pound makes play, of "rose—flamingo—iron rust—cherry" as the components of the Chinese ideogram for "red". Berkeley agrees with Fenollosa that it is absurd to think we "see" the thing common to roses, flamingos, iron rust and cherries, and then label this abstraction "red"; we *see*, not a quality common to these things, but *all these things, by virtue of what is common to them*. Similarly when we say "man" we do not see the abstraction what-all-men-have-in-common; we *see* a particular man (a tall one, perhaps, a straight and tawny one) standing as a sign for *all* men *by virtue of what they have in common*. When for the purposes of a theorem we have to imagine "triangle", we do not see an abstraction that is not scalene nor isosceles nor yet equilateral; we see a particular triangle (scalene, perhaps) serving as a sign for all triangles by virtue of what all triangles have in common.

Berkeley draws out the implications of this for language, or, as he prefers to put it (and here perhaps he *is* Cartesian), the way in which language has misled men into the doctrine of abstractions:

But to give a farther account how words came to produce the doctrine of abstract ideas, it must be observ'd that it's a receiv'd opinion, that language has no other end but the communicating our ideas, and that every significant name stands for an idea. This being so, and it being withall certain, that names, which yet are not thought altogether insignificant, do not always mark out particular conceivable ideas, it is straightway concluded that they stand for abstract notions. That there are many names in use amongst speculative men, which do not always suggest to others determinate, particular ideas, or in truth anything at all, is what no body will deny. And a little attention will discover, that it is not necessary (even in the strictest reasonings) significant names which stand for ideas shou'd, every time they are us'd, excite in the understanding the ideas they are made to stand for: in reading and discoursing names being for the most part used as letters are in *algebra*, in which thô a particular quantity be mark'd by each letter, yet to proceed right it is not requisite that in every step each letter suggest to your thoughts, that particular quantity it was appointed to stand for.

At this point we have come full circle on to T. E. Hulme:

> In prose as in algebra concrete things are embodied in signs or counters which are moved about according to rules, without being visualized at all in the process ... One only changes the X's and the Y's back into physical things at the end of the process.

Berkeley agrees, but he points out that "signs or counters" (he uses the counter metaphor himself elsewhere) are not "abstractions". On the contrary it is only when we see language as largely composed of such "counters", that we do away with the need for supposing a faculty of abstraction at all. Hence we can agree with Hulme that the language of poetry should not be "abstract", without having to agree that therefore it cannot be symbolic, like the language of algebra. A mathematical symbol is one thing; an abstraction is another.

What we get, in fact, from Berkeley, is just what St.-John Perse asked for in the language of poetry, a way of using words "as fiduciary symbols like coins as values of monetary exchange". And as we moved from Perse to Valéry's remarks about taking words on the run, having faith in them for the sake of articulating a context, so in Berkeley we find the same observation:

> In the ordinary affairs of life, any phrases may be retain'd, so long as they excite in us proper sentiments, or dispositions to act in such a manner as is necessary for our well-being, how false soever they may be, if taken in a strict and speculative sense. Nay this is unavoidable since, propriety being regulated by custom, language is suited to the received opinions which are not always the truest. Hence it is impossible even in the most rigid, philosophic reasonings, so far to alter the bent or genius of the tongue we speak, as never to give a handle for cavillers to pretend difficulties and inconsistencies. But a fair and ingenuous reader will collect the sense, from the scope and tenor and connexion of a discourse, making allowances for those unaccurate modes of speech, which use has made inevitable.

This injunction to collect the sense, from "the scope and tenor and connexion of a discourse", seems very like Dr. Leavis's advice not to dwell in or upon the exultations and influences and visionary "moments" of Wordsworth, but to keep hold of "that sober verse in which they are presented". And by "connexion" in a discourse, Berkeley must mean, among other things, syntax. As Coleridge saw, syntax can have a place in poetry only when poetry makes use of what Hulme denied to it, a language of counters, of fiduciary symbols.

Berkeley of course, in his observations on language, never offers an opinion on the peculiar sort of language (if it *is* peculiar) required for poetry. And we may well feel, as we surely must, that not all the words in a poem should be "fiduciary symbols". Indeed, we have found ourselves in the position of applauding nouns which are of this sort only because they allow of the use of verbs which vividly and distinctly mime the operation of an energy. But, again, we do not want all the nouns in our poetry to be like Wordsworth's "powers" and "influences"; we want, for objects as for actions, words which partake of the denseness and the tang of the things they stand for. Such words, or groups of words having this function, are loosely but usefully called, in our criticism, "images". And now that we have got rid of the bogey of "abstraction", finding that most apparently abstract words are in fact symbols, to be taken on trust, we are naturally led to wonder whether in poetry there may not be a right or normal ratio between words which are "signs" ("symbol" might be misleading here) and words which are "images".

Hulme and Fenollosa in effect admit into poetry no words that are not whole images or parts of images. This is one of the reasons why they tend to exclude syntax, for syntax always needs some words sheerly as signs. On the other hand, older poets and critics often insisted on the necessity for spacing images, sewing them carefully into language of another sort. As I have argued elsewhere, this is what I take Landor to mean, when he tells the poet:

> In every poem train the leading shoot;
> Break off the suckers. Thought erases thought,
> As numerous sheep erase each other's print
> When spungy moss they press or sterile sand.
> Blades thickly sown want nutriment and droop,
> Although the seed be sound, and rich the soil;
> Thus healthy-born ideas, bedded close,
> By dreaming fondness perish overlain.

Since Hulme and Fenollosa represent an influential tendency in the writing of verse, a tendency which their own influence in turn has helped to promote, it is now pertinent to examine the effect on poetic syntax of their refusal to countenance any words that are not "concrete". What happens to "the scope and tenor and connexion" of a poem, when the poet labours to give to every word the maximum concreteness?

§ 2

Among the words that looked like abstractions but were really fixed symbols, Berkeley included the word "I":

Euphranor. Pray tell me, Alciphron, is not an Idea altogether inactive? *Alciphron.* It is. *Euphranor.* An Agent therefore, an active Mind, or Spirit cannot be an Idea or like an Idea. Whence it shou'd seem to follow, that those Words which denote an active Principle, Soul, or Spirit do not, in a strict and proper Sense, stand for Ideas: And yet they are not insignificant neither: since I understand what is signified by the term *I*, or *my self*, or know what it means although it be no Idea, nor like an Idea, but that which thinks and wills and apprehends Ideas and operates about them.

It is easy to see that this conviction that the spiritual world is a world of action goes very deep with Berkeley, informing his own prose-style. It is what has recommended him to some modern thinkers, and it is what Yeats liked him for. In the wayward but very valuable Introduction that Yeats wrote for a book on Berkeley,[1] he declares, "Only where the mind partakes of a pure activity can art or life attain swiftness, volume, unity; . . ." And it is in the light of this that he makes the well-known comment on some of his contemporaries:

> One thinks of Joyce's *Anna Livia Plurabelle*, Pound's *Cantos*, works of an heroic sincerity, the man, his active faculties in suspense, one finger beating time to a bell sounding and echoing in the depths of his own mind; . . .

One brings this down to earth by rephrasing thus: the mind that is active produces poetry that finds room for verbs and hence (other things being equal) for syntax; when the active faculties are in suspense, the mind produces poetry that is crowded with "things", that finds little room for verbs, and either abjures syntax or retains only its empty forms.

This is a brutal simplification but it seems to work. Rosemond Tuve points out that Yeats differs from other poets of his generation precisely in the use he makes of syntax:

> Yeats's images are often more traditional than other modern poets' in method, as though in spite of his Symbolist alignments he felt the need of pointing a reader toward the significance "meant to be seen"—but few modern poets quite like to do this. This is one reason why there are few difficult images in Yeats in which the syntax does not repay study; syntax is the most unobtrusive of all methods of clarification, the closest one can come to the paradox of saying something tacitly[2].

It is natural to connect this with Richard Ellmann's comment on Yeats, in the light of his observation just quoted, about Joyce and Pound:

> His own way did not lie in the suspension of the active faculties; to the end he remained stubbornly loyal in his art to the conscious mind's intelligible structure.[3]

[1] *Bishop Berkeley: His Life, Writings, and Philosophy*, by J. M. Hone and M. M. Rossi, pp. xv-xxix.
[2] *Elizabethan and Metaphysical Imagery*, p. 177.
[3] "Joyce and Yeats", *Kenyon Review*, VII, 4, p. 636.

There is a road plainly open from the intelligible structure of the conscious mind to the intelligible structure of the sentence.

George Barnes supplies an example of Yeats's concern for syntax in his own work, when he recalls the poet's behaviour at a rehearsal for the broadcast reading of his poetry:

> ... at the rehearsal of a later programme when Baddeley read the first lines of "Sailing to Byzantium":
>
>> "That is no country for old men. The young
>> In one another's arms; birds in the trees . . ."
>
> Yeats exclaimed "Stop! That is the worst bit of syntax I ever wrote", and promptly changed it to:
>
>> "Old men should quit a country where the young
>> In one another's arms; birds in the trees . . ."[1]

This is a change which would have warmed the heart of Ernest Fenollosa. The copula and the negative are replaced by the energetic verb "quit". The syntax of the first version was correct enough; but by the revision the poem is given from the first line a backbone, a head and a tail, a drive to carry through the clutter of images that follow.

Just as Yeats abjured "free" syntax, so he abjured free-verse. And this was inevitable. For if Landor was right in thinking that images in a poem must be "spaced", then if the poet abandons the spacing he can get by syntax, he has to find some other means. Eliot and Pound find typography; the pause at the ends of lines or spaces in the middle of lines represent the interval which must be left by the reader between the impact of one image and the impact of another. Abolish syntax and you tend to abolish metre: free-verse becomes a necessity.

This is clearly seen if we examine a poet who crowds his images one upon another while retaining metre:

> Time, milk and magic, from the world beginning,
> Time is the tune my ladies lend their heartbreak,
> From bald pavilions and the house of bread
> Time tracks the sound of shape on man and cloud,
> On rose and icicle the ringing handprint.

[1] Quoted by Joseph Hone, *W. B. Yeats, 1865–1939*, p. 456.

These verses are quoted by Elizabeth Sewell, in a discussion of Rimbaud. She takes it as an example in English of what Rimbaud was doing in *Les Illuminations*:

> Coleridge ... says that images may have the function of "reducing multitude to unity, or succession to an instant". This fits well here, for Rimbaud, by the closely packed images of *Illuminations*, achieves that very thing, making the reader's mind discard its usual organization of words and images in small separate units, so that a new and far greater unity can be produced, a unity where everything in the cosmos runs into everything else in one enormous oneness, and in place of succession and similarity there only remain simultaneity in space-time, and identification.[1]

This means, in the terms we have been using, that Dylan Thomas exploits a pseudo-syntax. Formally correct, his syntax cannot mime, as it offers to do, a movement of the mind. If the effect is simultaneity and identification, these sentences that seem to drive forward in time through their verbs in fact do no such thing. The verb "tracks" is completely void of meaning. What appears to be narrative ("Time", the agent, transfers energy through "tracks" to the object "sound") is in fact an endless series of copulas: "Time is tracking which is sound which is shape ..." and so on. That the metaphors could in fact be broken down into successive meanings is irrelevant; even when the breaking down has been done for us, we cannot hold on to it when we return to reading the poem. This explains why Dylan Thomas's good poems are all written in complicated stanza-forms, where the varying lengths of line break down the images into "small separate units" which can be digested by the reader. In *A Refusal to Mourn the Death, by Fire, of a Child in London*, the stanza in print affords the same typographic breathing-spaces as a passage of free-verse. It goes without saying, of course, that in poems of any worth, the arrangement of type corresponds to an arrangement of rhythms. In free-verse and in Dylan Thomas's complicated metrical

[1] Elizabeth Sewell, *The Structure of Poetry*, p. 131.

stanzas the articulation and spacing of images is done by
rhythm instead of syntax; Thomas's sonnets, I think, show that
to do this the rhythms need to be far more various and more
strongly-marked than is possible in the decasyllabic line of the
traditional sonnet.

Revealing in this connection are two comments on Rimbaud's syntax which Miss Sewell puts side by side. C. A.
Hackett observes:

> One could claim that the poet deliberately suppresses the
> verbs to lighten the sentence and give more of a lift to his
> thought.[1]

And François Ruchon:

> The imagery with Rimbaud ... always envisages reality
> under the appearance of mobility; that is to say, the verb plays a
> predominant role in it.[2]

There is no contradiction here, if one critic is speaking of the
authentic syntax *behind* the verse, the other of the pseudo-
syntax it in fact employs. "Mobility", too, is significant. This
verse is often applauded for its energy, its "dynamic activity";
and this is just. But the energy is "wild", undifferentiated; its
verbs, any and all of them, are spurts or scurries of activity, a
restless fidget. Miss Sewell, endorsing this comment by
Ruchon, connects the "restlessness and mobility" of Rimbaud's verse in *Les Illuminations* with a characteristic of the
images of dream, the way they resist any effort to hold them
clear and steady. The dream-image is constantly changing.
This suggests the further observation that a sonnet by Dylan
Thomas is unacceptable even on Hulme's terms. When concrete images are crowded upon each other, they lose their concreteness. The milk is soured by the magic, the bread has lost
its tang and the cloud its volume. The things will not stand
still, but fluctuate and swim like weeds in a stream. A poem, it
seems, can give way under the weight of the "things" that are

[1] Elizabeth Sewell, *op cit.*, p. 127.
[2] *Ibid.*, p. 128.

crowded into it. Broken-backed, the poem can then no longer move; it can only twitch and flounder. Not only that; the things, tumbled pell-mell together, can no longer be identified:

> Thus healthy-born ideas, bedded close,
> By dreaming fondness perish overlain.

The poet who sets out to use only words partaking of the hardness and opacity of "things" finds in the end that the things have gone transparent and yielding. "Concreteness" itself, if we take it in its current signification, demands in metrical verse a language of "fixed symbols".

With free-verse the case is different. Here rhythm is set to do the work that syntax does in prose. But we can usefully recall here the notion of a contract between poet and reader. For syntax to be used in verse, the reader has to grant something to the poet—he has to agree to let some words pass in the reading, in the faith that their articulated context will give them the meaning they seem to lack in isolation. A poet who abandons syntax makes no such claim. But he makes other infinitely larger:

> ... I believe in an absolute rhythm. I believe that every emotion and every phase of emotion has some toneless phrase, some rhythm-phrase to express it.
>
> (This belief leads to *vers libre* and to experiments in quantitative verse.)[1]

Honest as ever, Pound reveals clearly the terms of the compact he would make with his reader. For it is plain that the reader has to make a like act of faith before he can yield himself to the *Cantos*. In the elaborate stanzas of Dylan Thomas at his best, we are not asked for as much as this. There the rhythms take on significance as they depart from or approach a metrical norm. But in Pound's verse the rhythm steps out alone and we must follow it in blind faith, with no metrical landmarks to assist us. Every reader must decide for himself whether he can make this

[1] *Gaudier-Brzeska, a Memoir*, p. 97.

act of faith. I confess for my part I cannot, and it seems to me that after scrapping the contracts traditionally observed between poet and reader, a poet like Pound substitutes a contract unjustly weighted against the reader.

But when we recognize Pound's and Eliot's honesty, we can give to that word as much weight as we like. Having banished syntax from their poetry, they do not pretend anything else. They do not mislead their readers by retaining even the empty shells of syntactical form. Such forms appear in their poetry, for instance in the weaving together of linguistic units which yet, in the scheme of the whole poem, stand in non-syntactical relation to other such units (as in *Four Quartets*); and when this happens, the syntax is authentic in a way that Rimbaud's is not. Rimbaud's syntax, on this showing, is really a pseudo-syntax, a play of forms without even that recondite truthfulness that Mrs. Langer claims for her syntax like music. Pseudo-syntax of this kind appears to me to be radically vicious; in the sense, at least, that where it appears poetry flies out of the door. Elizabeth Sewell, I gather, would not disagree.

Finally I think there is force in Peter Allt's suggestion that, where authentic syntax appears in modern poetry, it is a sort of tribute[1] paid by the poet to "the beautiful humane cities". Systems of syntax are part of the heritable property of past civilization, and to hold firm to them is to be traditional in the best and most important sense. This seems ungracious to both Pound and Eliot, who have both insisted upon the value of the European civilized tradition, and have tried to embody it in their poems. Nevertheless, it is hard not to agree with Yeats that the abandonment of syntax testifies to a failure of the poet's nerve, a loss of confidence in the intelligible structure of the conscious mind, and the validity of its activity.

[1] Peter Allt, "Yeats, Religion and History", *Sewanee Review*, LX, 4.

XI

SYNTAX, RHETORIC, AND RHYME

꒫꒫꒫꒫꒫꒫꒫꒫꒫꒫꒫꒫꒫꒫꒫꒫꒫꒫꒫꒫꒫꒫꒫꒫꒫꒫꒫꒫꒫꒫

S IR PHILIP SIDNEY maintained that it was the privilege
and peculiar glory of poetry to get the best of both worlds,
of history on the one hand, of philosophy on the other.
This insight has been elaborated as follows by Mr. Northrop
Frye:[1]

> History gives the example of the hero without the precept;
> Philosophy the precept without the example, and poetry gives us
> the poetic image of the hero which combines the two. Or, as we
> may say, literature, being hypothetical, unites the temporal event
> with the idea in conceptual space. On one side, it develops a
> narrative interest which borders on history; on the other, a dis-
> cursive interest which borders on philosophy, and in between
> them is its central interest of imagery.
>   We may thus distinguish three main rhythms of literature and
> three main areas of it, one in which narrative controls the rhythm,
> one in which a discursive interest controls it, and a central area
> in which the image controls it. This central area is the area of
> poetry; the parietal ones belong to prose, which is used for both
> hypothetical and descriptive purposes.

Mr. Frye then relates each of these "three main rhythms" and
"three main areas" to one of the three departments of the
trivium. Philosophy, with its discursive rhythm based on the

[1] "Levels of Meaning in Literature", *Kenyon Review*, XII, 2, pp. 246–
262.

unit of the proposition, falls in the department of logic; poetry, with its figurative rhythm (based on "the arranging and patterning of verbal symbols"), in the province of rhetoric; and history, with its narrative rhythm, in the province of grammar.

It is this last alignment, no doubt, that at first appears peculiar. Yet Fenollosa has made it already. For Mr. Frye is echoing Fenollosa when he writes:

> As for narrative prose, it is clear that we cannot restrict the conception of narrative to the gross events: the basis of narrative is the temporal order of symbols; in particular, the word-order which is the movement of literature. We may, then, suggest a link between narrative and grammar . . .

This is precisely Fenollosa's insight by which every sentence is seen to have a plot. It seems that for Mr. Frye this perception is less important than it was for Fenollosa, and it may be that he gives it less importance than he should—a point to which I shall return. On the other hand, his appeal to the trivium (grammar, rhetoric, logic) seems to explain what is wrong with Fenollosa's principles when we try to apply them in criticism. If Mr. Frye is right in sending us back to the trivium, then Fenollosa's essay represents an attempt to climb into poetry up one of its props, that of history, narrative and grammar, while taking away the prop on the other side, that of philosophy, the discursive and logical.

For instance, we may compare with Fenollosa's dislike of the copula, of what he calls the "weak" (meaning "unpoetic") *is*, Mr. Frye's reminder about "the metaphysical structures based on the fact that the verb *to be* implies both existence and identity." So Jonson starts a poem:

> To know no vice at all and keep true state
> Is virtue and not fate; . . .

and we get an effect of tremendous rapidity, as if the sense were a ball-bearing that pelts along a slot and raps upon the metal check of the rhyme. For this effect of energy there is nothing in

Fenollosa's essay to prepare us. Innocent of all concretion, and driving through the so-called "weak" copula, the line should have no energy at all and, in isolation, no poetic value. In fact it seems to me that it has both, and leaving aside all questions of metre and the tone of address, I find that energy in syntax, pre-eminently in the twin implications of the verb *to be*: the lines have the effect of proclaiming exultantly that this innocence exists, at the same time as they make a predication about it. A verb capable of doing so much must be, for all that Fenollosa says to the contrary, a channel of great energy.

Mr. Frye, when he writes that literature "unites the temporal event with the idea in conceptual space", is, in effect, challenging Fenollosa in Fenollosa's own terms. For the latter's insistence on narrative came from his insistence that all mental experience occurs in the dimension of time and (this is his implication) *in that alone*. Yet while this may be true of our perception of a man seeing a horse ("We saw, first, the man before he acted; second, while he acted; third, the object toward which his action was directed"), is it true of our perceptions of corre-spondences, identities, or incongruities (such as provoke for instance a burst of laughter)? Of these we are accustomed to say that we saw them "in a flash", and this witnesses to our feeling that these perceptions occur out of time, in no time at all. Every thinker will testify, for instance, to the way in which, having laboured over two bodies of evidence, having followed repeatedly the steps in each of them, having tugged them about and measured them against each other, he sees the connection between them suddenly, "in a flash". There is obviously a connection between the process of "mulling over" and the final recognition. But the connection remains mysterious, and perception in the end seems not a working from the one thing to the other, rather, a seeing of them simultaneously side by side. They are "side by side", I take it, in Mr. Frye's "con-ceptual space", in a dimension of mental activity which is other than Fenollosa's temporal dimension, and one for which his theory finds no room. If we want to transmit our perception to another, we cast it in temporal form, with all the verbs that Fenollosa requires: "If we pursue this line of argument . . .", "It follows that . . .", "We reach the conclusion . . .". But here the time-dimension is a falsification, not a true rendering of the way the perception came to us; for it is characteristic of this type of perception that it comes to us, we do not go after it and seize it.

Mr. Frye returns to "conceptual space" when he writes:

> The link between rhetoric and logic, between the image and the concept, is in the diagrammatic structures underneath our thoughts, which appear in the spatial metaphors we use. "Beside", "on the other hand", "upon", "outside": nobody could connect thoughts at all without such words, yet every one is a geometrical image, and suggests that every concept has its graphic formula.[1]

This is unsatisfactory, if only because Fenollosa, arguing from Chinese, in which "the preposition is frankly a verb", has speculated whether, in English too, prepositions are not verbal in origin. At all events, in the examples that Mr. Frye gives, "on the other hand" could well be regarded as shorthand for a movement of turning from one side to another, as "upon" for an act of placing, and "outside" for an act of exclusion, the shutting of a door in the stranger's face. In other words, these prepositions and prepositional phrases could be the images of actions in time no less than arrangements in space.

But what worries me, in Mr. Frye's account of "the link between rhetoric and logic", is the inference that may be drawn from it, that logical discourse is permissible in poetry only when the metaphors it uses, whether spatial and passive, or temporal and active, come to life in the reading. This is an implication common to both Mr. Frye and Fenollosa. For the

---

[1] Cf. Bergson: "We think in terms of space—the insurmountable difficulties presented by certain philosophic problems arise from the fact that we separate out in space, phenomena which do not occupy space" (quoted by Hulme, *Speculations*, p. 178). But contrast P. Wyndham Lewis, *Time and Western Man*, p. 3.

latter, too, language becomes true and poetic only when it brings again to life the metaphors gone dead in abstractions:

> Only scholars and poets feel painfully back along the thread of our etymologies and piece together our diction, as best they may, from forgotten fragments. This anaemia of modern speech is only too well encouraged by the feeble cohesive force of our phonetic symbols. There is little or nothing in a phonetic word to exhibit the embryonic stages of its growth. It does not bear its metaphor on its face. We forget that personality once meant, not the soul, but the soul's mask. This is the sort of thing one can not possibly forget in using the Chinese symbols.[1]

Of course I agree. I agree that one half of the poet's task "lies in feeling back along the lines of advance", as I agree with Pound in a footnote that the other half is to "prepare for new advances along the lines of true metaphor". But there is also the question of strategy, of where and how to create the new metaphor or re-create the old, so that it may have the greatest effect. The right strategy is not to reveal the metaphor, the concretion, in every word used, even in prepositions like "upon" or "outside". This is the strategy of some poets writing today; and the result is only an incessant and intolerable fidget. If all the words we use are dead or dormant metaphors, then in any one poem the poet must permit the greater part of such words to continue sleeping or shamming dead. Only in that way can he bring into prominence the metaphors he has for the moment selected to create or to re-create. The language of logical discourse is chiefly valuable to the poet for providing a store of such words that can be left as "fiduciary symbols":

> Ev'ry thy haire for love to worke upon
> Is much too much, some fitter must be sought;
> For, nor in nothing, nor in things
> Extreme, and scatt'ring bright, can love inhere;
> Then as an Angell, face, and wings
> Of aire, not pure as it, yet pure doth weare,

[1] Fenollosa, *op. cit.*, pp. 74, 75.

So thy love may be my loves spheare;
    Just such disparitie
As is 'twixt Aire and Angells puritie,
'Twixt womens love, and mens will ever bee.

Here the only concretion is the image of the aureole of hair—
"ev'ry thy haire ... extreme, and scatt'ring bright"; and the
only re-created metaphor occurs in conjunction with this, in
"extreme". The words of logical discourse, such as "inhere"
and "disparitie", or even (given the philosophy Donne has in
mind) such words as "Angell", "aire" and "spheare", are not
subjected to the same probing beam, but taken at their face-
value, marshalled rapidly into the analogical structure, and
used as pegs for the syntactical weave. If Donne had given
concreteness to "spheare", for instance (as of course he was to
do in other poems), that would only have got in his way, dis-
tracting the reader's attention. If the word "spheare" had
thickened into a thing rather than a fiduciary symbol, it would
have grown too dense and heavy, tearing a hole in the web the
poet weaves about it.

I am equally unhappy about the other of Mr. Frye's "links":

The link between grammar and rhetoric appears to be a subconscious paronomasia, or free association among words, from
which there arise not only semantic connections, but the more
arbitrary resemblances in sound out of which the schemata
of rhyme and assonance evolve. *Finnegans Wake* is an attempt
to write a whole book on this level, and it draws heavily on
the researches of Freud and Jung into subconscious verbal
association.

Mr. Frye illustrates from Smart's *Jubilate Agno* what he
describes as "the creative process in an interesting formative
stage":

For the power of some animal is predominant in every language.
For the power and spirit of a CAT is in the Greek.
The sound of a cat is in the most useful preposition
    Kat'euchen ...

135

and he goes on:

> It is possible that similar sputters and sparks of the fusing intellect take place in all poetic thinking. The puns in this passage impress the reader as both outrageous and humorous, which is consistent with Freud's view of wit as the escape of impulse from the control of the censor. In creation the impulse appears to be the creative energy itself, and the censor the force which adapts that impulse to outward expression, a force which might be called the "plausibility-principle".

This is undoubtedly well said; one only doubts if this was the place to say it. For we are forced to ask what connection there is between this paronomasia and the "grammar" we have been invited to see as the province of narrative, of energy transferred from agent through active verb to object. Fenollosa's view of the link between grammar and rhetoric has the advantage of holding close to this perception of plot in the sentence, and I think it is preferable.

I have dwelt upon this essay by Northrop Frye because it seems to me an exceptionally subtle and intelligent statement of a view which is widely held. As Mr. Frye rightly maintains, it was held also by the Elizabethans. The argument goes something like this: rhetoric is the province of poetry, as logic is the province of discourse, and grammar the province of narrative; rhetoric touches upon and even overlaps grammar on the one side, logic on the other; but logic and grammar move into the area of rhetoric, history and philosophy move into poetry, *only by shedding their distinctive syntax*. The forms of discursive and narrative syntax may be retained, in accordance with "the plausibility-principle"; but in that case the forms are empty and fraudulent, for articulation in rhetoric and poetry is not by syntax but by figuration of images.

§ 2

The case for rhetoric can be made more subtly still. The argument goes as follows. Words are not signs standing for ideas, but it is important to behave as if they were. Fortunately this behaviour and this illusion appear to be endemic in man. The illusion that words are signs for ideas is invaluable, because it means that the mind when it hears a word said will look for an idea to fit it. If it cannot find such an idea to stand as "meaning" or reference, it will make one. Or so it seems; but in fact the idea must somehow have been there, waiting to be made—as Northrop Frye says, "the poet's new poem merely articulates what was already latent in the order of words." Loosely, however, we may say that the word creates the idea, creates its own meaning. And the practical injunction arising from this argument is clear: "Do not be afraid of using a meaningless word; use it, and the meaning will accrue to it."

Jean Paulhan gives two striking examples:

> Cilia, when attempting to explain to the doctor what ails her little daughter, comes to realize as she speaks what she really fears, and is astonished at herself. When Atys finds himself saying to Chrysos: "So you lied", each of them, starting from the word, composes his thought afresh. An idea here serves as a sign to the word, and as a means of sharing it, far from the word being so for the idea. We know, too, of the poet who, cast among words, squeezes them, listens to them, awaits them.[1]

We all know this common experience: "I had spoken, before I realized what I was saying." And perhaps most poets can testify to the way an apparently meaningless line of verse will arise in the mind, demanding a context that shall make sense of it.

Here the word is a sign, only after it has been uttered; it calls into being the idea to fit it. Hence (so the argument develops), if we make patterns of words, patterns of thought (of experience) will follow. Make a syntactical structure, and a structure in nature, psychical or even physical, will be found to leap towards it. In this way the inconceivable becomes conceivable. Because we want a perfect language, a language fitting words

[1] Jean Paulhan, "Jacob Cow the Pirate", in *Essays on Language and Literature*, ed. Hevesi, p. 114.

closely to reality, our language becomes perfect even as we use it. And all syntax becomes authentic ("true") as soon as it has been constructed. This, I think, is what Rimbaud meant:

Du reste, toute parole étant idée, le temps d'un langage universel viendra.

Every word *is* an idea. It is not just a sign for an idea. For if there was no idea for it to signify before it was uttered, as soon as it was uttered the idea awoke to meet it.

But there are in language systems of articulation other than syntax. There is, in particular, the articulation indicated by the "figures auricular" of the old rhetoric-books, the relations that words strike up among themselves by similarities of sound or written appearance, relations known to us as metre, quantity, alliteration, assonance, rhyme. If we are to trust words to do our thinking for us (and we have shown that we may and do— by articulating themselves, words articulate thoughts), we must trust them when they make this sort of pattern, no less than when they make the patterns we call syntactical.

So Paulhan writes:

Much is said of the spell of rhyme: perhaps for want of reasons. It does not disconcert us, but indeed falls exactly in with the line of our comments, that the task of this rhyme should be to provide grounds momentarily for a claim by proximity in sound to proximity in sense—and so to gratify our concern for a perfect language. We should not accuse it on occasion of hindering the meaning if we had not counted on its helping it. We experience this disappointment because we entertained that hope.[1]

Is this really the task of rhyme, and its effect when successful —to persuade us that when words sound alike they must mean alike?

H. M. McLuhan selects two lines by Pope to illustrate how the couplet can contrive a main plot and a sub-plot:

> The hungry judges soon the sentence sign
> And wretches hang that jurymen may dine.

[1] Paulhan, *loc. cit.*, pp. 119, 120.

Here there is proximity in sense in so far as (the rhyme suggests) the signing of a death-warrant and eating one's dinner are actions equally momentous to the coarsened and dehumanized mind. But here the rhyme only clinches an effect prepared by the syntax; if the sub-plot is a parallel to the main plot, obviously the climax of the one is likely to resemble the climax of the other. And this is only a particularly obvious example. Professor W. K. Wimsatt, in a sustained and admirable analysis of Pope's rhyming, shows that such an exercise becomes inevitably an analysis of syntax—"In fact, words have no character as rhymes, until they become points in a syntactic succession."[1] In other words, articulation by rhyme depends upon syntax as much as articulation by images.

If this were not so, there would be no difference between rhyme and other relationships by sound that the words set up among themselves. Then Smart's lunatic logic (quoted by Mr. Frye) would be cogent:

> For two creatures the Bull and the Dog prevail in the English,
> For all the words ending in ble are in the creature.
> Invisi-ble, Incomprehensi-ble, ineffa-ble, A-ble . . .
> For there are many words under Bull . . .
> For Brook is under Bull. God be gracious to Lord Bolingbroke.

All that differentiates this from such an exercise in "figures auricular" as Sidney's "Shepherd's Song" is the absence of what Mr. Frye calls the "plausibility-principle". And that, so we are to understand, is in any case optional, only a sop to the reader's prosaic habits.

Again we perceive that rhetorical theories of poetry demand of the reader an enormous initial act of faith. Jean Paulhan's argument has the effect of giving enormous weight to the first word in the phrase "fiduciary symbol". And when we look back at them from this point, St.-John Perse and Valéry appear in a different light. The possibility now presents itself that

---

[1] W. K. Wimsatt, "One Relation of Rhyme to Reason", in *The Verbal Icon* (University of Kentucky Press, 1954), p. 156.

when they asked us to have faith in words as symbols, they were asking for far more than Berkeley, for instance, who at one time seemed to echo them.

And yet we have to admit the force of Jean Paulhan's anecdote about Cilia and her little girl who is sick. It is true that a word, once uttered, can evoke a meaning that flies to meet it; that sometimes and quite legitimately in our common speech the word comes first and the idea, the appropriate meaning, only afterwards. C. Day Lewis point out that this is implicit in two well-known manifestos in verse written by poets in English, Edward Thomas's "English Words", and the passage from "Little Gidding" which begins, "So here I am, in the middle way . . .":

> Both poets speak of words as if they had an independent life of their own ("Choose me, you English words": "one has only learnt to get the better of words"). Both poets are expressing a sense of dedication and of humility: Mr. Eliot writes of the "men whom one cannot hope to emulate"; Edward Thomas asks words to use him "As the winds use a crack in the wall or a drain". Both poets consider a poem as an exploration—"a raid on the inarticulate", Mr. Eliot calls it—in which words play the leading part, can discover truths the poet was unaware of or incredulous of—"as dear as the earth which *you prove* that we love".[1]

This seems to imply, once again, that no arrangement of words can ever, strictly speaking, be meaningless. And so it reinforces Jean Paulhan's plea for "the rhetorician", who has faith that words will lead him to truth, as opposed to "the terrorist", who suspects that words are always ready to baffle and mislead unless he keeps control of them.

Yet Mr. Eliot speaks of "getting the better of words", and he says he proceeds "By strength and submission"—by submission certainly, but also by strength, by letting the words lead him, but also by making them go where he wants. This, I

[1] C. Day Lewis, "What is Modern Poetry?" *The Listener*, Jan. 22, 1953, p. 148.

should say, is in part what makes Mr. Eliot's lines superior to Thomas's. He grasps the paradox of poetic composition, its way of surrendering and conquering all at once. According to Mr. Eliot (and of course corroboration can be found), the poet's traffic with the words he uses induces in him a state of mind that is neither passive nor active, but both, and both at once. If this is so, then the distinction between "terrorist" and "rhetorician" is false: for the poet, it seems, in the act of composition, is both. And the active positive element in the affair is something more essential than a graceful acquiescence in Professor Frye's "plausibility-principle"; it is what we come across in Yeats, a declaration of faith in the conscious mind, its intelligible structure and significant activity.

XII

THE GRAMMARIAN'S FUNERAL

ᚖᚖᚖᚖᚖᚖᚖᚖᚖᚖᚖᚖᚖᚖᚖᚖᚖᚖᚖᚖᚖᚖᚖ

J ESPERSEN'S investigations into the historical development
of English grammar have been seen to invalidate some of
the presumptions about "concreteness" which are still
current among poets and their readers. The upshot of his arguments was that the only ultimate concretion is "the experience";
and that the "things", so much prized by many poets and
critics for their supposed concreteness, are in fact *abstractions*,
abstracted from experiences in which things, and the thoughts
and feelings they occasioned, were indistinguishable. T. E.
Hulme and his disciples could thereafter continue to ask poetry
for "things", rendered in all their toughness and quiddity; but
they could no longer pretend that, in making this demand, they
were appealing for a return to nature, to the original and as
they thought perennial norms of experiencing, obscured and
sophisticated by the refinements of grammarians and logicians.
To some of them, at any rate, this had been one of the strongest
attractions of the discredited doctrine of "concretion", its claim
to return to the archaic simplicity of a Golden Age which
poetry, if it were concrete enough, could re-create.

But Jespersen, in turn, lent himself to just this primitivism.
The return to nature was still a possibility, and it could be still
peculiarly the province of poetry to effect this return. It was
only necessary to change the poetic strategy. Owen Barfield
was the first English critic to realize this, and to demand of

poetry that it re-create the massive indivisible experiences of primitive man, for whom no distinction was possible between the things he perceived, the significances folded in those things, and the responses they evoked from him. I do not know that any critics have followed Mr. Barfield's lead. But certainly some poets have, or, if they have not, they have reached the same position by another route:

AFTERNOON AT HOME

Seeing the earth dry into shoots of summer
And sea dissolve the line of rock in steam
On my garden hill I gather
Impressions of the girl I live in dream

Until the ray that reads this flesh withdraws
Either from rare rainshine or dull moonwater
Drives me to pines with claws
And deserts the mere man who does not dream.

Under this granite bank fall banks of flowers
Lawns of herbs, grazing cubes of sea
Polished from hill to shore by showers
That release zones of new translucency

Where opaque dust, dazzling diamonds lay
Battering my sense to feel no symbol, no time,
Merely hostile rain, sepia spray-water,
In my Irish garden a grove of Japanese trees

Where rhododendron folly and quartz contour
Imposed foreign forms on day
Wrapped the night in snow-coral sea-fog,
Until I am not man or girl or dream

But wake from sleep this afternoon apart
Stretched on my garden rock an eye in words
Alone, to hear my song sung by birds,
Joined to hill, ground and sea, but separate.[1]

[1] Richard Murphy, *The Listener*, April 9, 1953.

The last five lines of this poem, so far as I understand them, come near to admitting that what is attempted in the whole is the re-creation of an experience in which the scene, the circumstances, and the mind of the protagonist swim into one another, from which nothing, not even the "I" and the "not-I", is abstracted.

Mr. Murphy dislocates his syntax. But it is perhaps not clear why he had to do so, his objective being what it was. Indeed, have I not claimed to show that Wordsworth's syntax in *The Prelude* was both authentic and poetic, just because he held close by experience, the ultimate concretion, in just this way? But alas, I fear Owen Barfield would not take *The Prelude* on my terms, any more than Ernest Fenollosa would. The thinness of Wordsworth's nouns would be immediately suspect. He too, it might be said, renders, not the experience itself, but an abstraction from it, an abstraction not of "things", but of everything else, everything that excludes the things. And I suppose I have to agree. Nothing will do, really, but the language of *Finnegans Wake*, or else Fenollosa's dream of an English like Chinese, where nouns are verbs, and verbs are nouns, and all other parts of speech are both and neither.

For if Fenollosa fell foul of Jespersen in the matter of metaphor, this other side of his argument is a surprising achievement of historical anticipation. He anticipates here not the poetic theorists but the grammarians themselves. For the grammarians soon realized, following Jespersen's line of thought, that the traditional English grammar, with its "parts of speech", could no longer apply. Terms such as "noun", "verb", "adverb", "preposition", themselves represent a breaking-down of the massive compounds of experience into thoroughly misleading "elements". They represent the imposition of a Latinate system upon modern European languages, where it does not fit. Hence, for instance, the traditional objection to the split infinitive can no longer be sustained. For "to walk" is not in any real sense the infinitive form of the verb "walk"; to regard it so is only a grammarian's convenience.

The whole of traditional grammar was thus thrown into the melting-pot:

> It is very doubtful whether English has a passive voice at all, in any meaningful sense of the term. "Mr. X is now being issued with a licence" might be bad Latin, but it is perfectly good English.[1]

It depends what we mean by "good". No doubt we have to agree with Mr. Hugh Sykes Davies that it is entirely *correct* English (if, that is, as grammar now stands, the terms "correct" and "incorrect" still have any meaning at all). But it does not follow that the purist, when he objected to that construction, was moved only by feelings of vindictive superiority. Nor does it follow that the ground has now been cut from under his feet. He feels, perhaps, not the nasty meanness of a pedant, but the same pang of angry discomfort as he feels before any kind of tastelessness—in stone and steel, no less than in words. What matters, surely, is that this construction is ugly, inelegant. Ideas of beauty and elegance differ, no doubt; but mine are not therefore any less real, for me and perhaps for others.

And up to a point they can be rationalized. Beauty is, or it includes, order; ugliness is or includes muddle. "Mr. X is being issued with a licence"; "rum is being issued with a ladle". The connection between "Mr. X" and his "licence" is quite different, in quite another pattern, from the connection between the rum and the ladle. If these two different patterns are cast into one pattern of speech, somewhere there is muddle; and muddle is ugly. It is also dishonest, for a distinction in experience is being denied in the speech that claims to render it.

This is beside the point. If the grammarian has got into the position of condoning muddle, that is the grammarian's funeral. What matters to us is the effect of these trains of thought upon poetry. It has for long been acknowledged that the poet enjoys a special licence in the matter of making nouns do the work of verbs, adjectives of nouns, and so on. There

---

[1] "Thersites", "Private Views", *The Irish Times*, April 11, 1953.

are abundant examples in Shakespeare. But now it can be claimed that this sort of thing is at the very heart of poetry, since it represents a re-creation by the poet of the natural patterns of experience. Allen Tate begins a poem:

> The idiot greens the meadow with his eyes.

and his poem ends,

> the towering weak and pale
> Covers his eyes with memory like a sheet.

The adjective "green" serves as a verb; other adjectives, "towering", "weak", "pale", serve, some or all of them, as nouns. And of course the device is not uncommon. Richard Murphy's poem represents only a more extreme and less efficient application of the same principle—but with this difference. Allen Tate's poem is about an idiot, and it tries to re-create faithfully the patterns of idiotic experience. To identify the primitive with the natural, and the natural with the genuine, is to imply that the idiot is the only honest man. We reach the point where to write poetry or to read it, we have to behave like idiots.

XIII

WHAT IS MODERN POETRY?

HAT is modern poetry? We cannot say, simply, that all poets who have written since a specific date are thereby modern poets. Or rather, we can talk of "modern poetry" in this sense, but more often we do not. Mr. Walter De La Mare is presumably a modern poet in this sense, but his is not the poetry we have in mind when we speak of "modern" poetry. Usually when we use the term, we have in mind poetry which has broken with the poetry of our grandfathers in a way that Mr. De La Mare's exquisite poetry has not. "Modern", in fact, has taken over the functions of the now outmoded adjective "modernist"; modern poetry, as we usually understand it, is something that appears aggressively and consciously different, in important ways, from the poetry of the past. In this sense of "modern", the modern poet is standing on the near side of a gulf. Very often, indeed, the poet is at some pains to show us that the gulf can be bridged, and he points to the bridges he has crossed. But at any rate the bridges are thrown over in unlikely places; they are not broad and obvious like the bridge that leads back from Mr. De La Mare to Keats.

All the same, the bridges are easier to find than is the gulf beneath them. Or rather, the gulf is plain when we are "on the spot", and very deep and wide; but it is hard to find it on the map or to instruct the stranger where to look out for it. There is a distinct break with the past, that we know; there is a gulf to be crossed if we want to move from Tennyson to T. S. Eliot; but when we try to define that break, to chart the gulf, we fall out among ourselves. We have all negotiated the passage, yet it seems we have come by different routes. One party of poets and critics finds the decisive innovation in one place, another in quite another, and so on. And though we feel, viewing the matter from a distance, that all modern poetry hangs together, when we come closer this impression vanishes and we see only a bewildering diversity. Somehow, we acknowledge, modern poetry begins with symbolism. Modern poetry, we say, is post-symbolist poetry. *Post hoc*, certainly, but *propter hoc*? And there we begin to wrangle. It is just there, when we try to explain just *how* symbolism "started it all", that we fall out.

If the foregoing pages have tended to any one conclusion it is this: the break with the past is at bottom a change of attitude towards poetic syntax. It is from that point of view, in respect of syntax, that modern poetry, so diverse in all other ways, is seen as one. And we can define it thus: *What is common to all modern poetry is the assertion or the assumption (most often the latter) that syntax in poetry is wholly different from syntax as understood by logicians and grammarians.* When the poet retains syntactical forms acceptable to the grammarian, this is merely a convention which he chooses to observe. We may acknowledge that such emptied forms are to be found (and frequently too) in Shakespeare and in Milton. But never before the modern period has it been taken for granted that all poetic syntax is necessarily of this sort.

This is, surely, the one symbolist innovation that is at the root of all the other technical novelties that the symbolist poets introduced. Later poets could refuse to countenance all the other symbolist methods and still, by sharing, consciously or not, the symbolist attitude to syntax, they stand out as patently "post-symbolist". This aspect of the symbolist doctrine—and, as I have pointed out, it is more than just one aspect, it is at the core—has been obscured by the fact that Mallarmé and

Valéry talk of syntax, and appear to lay great store by it, in a way that earlier poets did not. But this arises from the use of one word "syntax" to mean two things which are really widely different. In fact I think we shall find that we need, not just two terms, but several, instead of the one. At any rate, Mallarmé and Valéry, when they speak of "syntax", do not mean by it what is meant by the common reader.

Here only blunt common sense will serve:

> The point was not that the emotions of, say, Jules Laforgue were necessarily more complicated than those of, say, Catullus in his sequence of poems about Lesbia, but rather than the symbolist poet—instead of disentangling a complex emotion into a series of varying moods or at least, when the mood of a single poem is allowed to change abruptly (as in Catullus's *Illa Lesbia* ...), of subduing the disordered feeling to the logic of consecutive statement—is in the habit of telescoping the whole thing by a few stenographic strokes. Nor are his feelings necessarily more difficult to render than those, say, of Wordsworth in the most mysterious of his visions of the natural world; but the symbolist—instead of attempting to reduce an unearthly elusive sensation to the lucidity of simple language—invents for it a vocabulary and a syntax as unfamiliar as the sensation itself.[1]

The symbolist poet, we realize, has a choice of two alternatives: either he telescopes his feeling "by a few stenographic strokes" —that is, he abandons even the appearance of syntactical arrangement and merely juxtaposes images; or else he "invents ... a syntax as unfamiliar as the sensation itself"—that is, something that may look like normal syntax but fulfils a quite different function.

As H. M. McLuhan has pointed out, Wordsworth comes nearest to symbolist poetry in such a poem as "The Solitary Reaper", where he leaves the reader to gather from the poem the feeling, never overtly described, which inspired the poet to write it. This is the poetry of "the objective correlative", which

---

[1] Edmund Wilson, *The Shores of Light*, pp. 55, 56.

describes, not the emotion itself, but a symbolic landscape or action which may stand as its equivalent.[1] It is sometimes maintained that the discovery how to do this was the decisive innovation of the symbolists, and the starting-point for the symbolist movement. But this is not the case, as the reference to Wordsworth serves to show. What is novel in symbolist technique is the way of organizing the items inside the symbolic landscape or the train of symbolic events.

When Edmund Wilson points out that Tennyson "was nearer to the school of Verlaine than it is likely to occur to us to notice", he is enforcing this point, that the objective correlative is not peculiar to symbolism but can be found in pre-symbolist writing. Tennyson indeed is a crucial case, and H. M. McLuhan has treated him at some length from this point of view, arguing that he anticipates the Symbolist expedient of "*le paysage intérieur* or the psychological landscape":

> This landscape, by means of discontinuity, which was first developed in picturesque painting, effected the apposition of widely diverse objects as a means of establishing what Mr. Eliot has called "an objective correlative" for a state of mind... Whereas in external landscape diverse things lie side by side, so in psychological landscape the juxtaposition of various things and experiences becomes a precise musical means of orchestrating that which could never be rendered by systematic discourse. Landscape is the means of presenting, without the copula of logical enunciation, experiences which are united in existence but not in conceptual thought. Syntax becomes music, as in Tennyson's "Mariana".[2]

[1] Cf. Yvor Winters, "Gerard Manley Hopkins", *Kenyon Review*, Vol. II, No. 1, p. 63: "In no other literary period, I think, would a poet who was both a priest and a genuinely devout man have thought that he had dealt seriously with his love for Christ and his duty toward Him by writing an excited description of a landscape: this kind of thing belongs to the nineteenth and twentieth centuries, to the period of self-expression and the abnegation of reason."

[2] H. M. McLuhan, "Tennyson and Picturesque Poetry" *Essays in Criticism*, I, 3, pp. 270, 271.

"Syntax becomes music"; and this is plainly the "music" of St.-John Perse, which is best fitted for "joining without binding, and gathering together without fettering". It is the music of Suzanne Langer, in which "The actual function of meaning, which calls for permanent contents, is not fulfilled; for the *assignment* of one rather than another possible meaning to each form is never explicitly made." And if our earlier analysis was correct, this means a syntax that is a shadow-play, a lifting of non-existent weights, a dance that ends where it began.

It will have been noticed that Wilson and McLuhan differ at one point, radically. For the latter the symbolist sort of syntax is justified because by it the poet may communicate or embody "that which could never be rendered by systematic discourse". And this is something that Wilson goes out of his way to deny. Laforgue, he insists, could have been as systematic as Catullus; he chose not to be:

> Symbolism, at its most successful, contrives to communicate emotions by images whose connection with the subject and whose relevance to one another we may not always understand ... These images could probably have been conveyed in a perfectly conventional manner—as Dante, describing a state of mind surely not less unusual and difficult, would write in the *Paradiso* of the fading from his memory of the divine vision, "so the snow is unsealed by the sun, so the light leaves of the Sybil's message are scattered by the wind."[1]

If Wilson is right, then McLuhan's case for symbolism comes out of a loss of faith in conceptual thought. It testifies to a loss of nerve, as with Hofmannsthal's Lord Chandos. And this was general. As Richard Ellmann says, Yeats stands almost alone in the post-symbolist generations as "stubbornly loyal in his art to the conscious mind's intelligible structure." For that, we see again, is what it amounts to: where there is authentic syntax in poetry (syntax, that is, not wholly different from the syntax of logician and grammarian), the poet retains hope of the

---

[1] Wilson, *loc. cit.*

conscious mind's activity; when he has lost that hope, his syntax is either dislocated altogether, or else turns into music.

H. M. McLuhan distinguishes between "picturesque" and "symbolist" poetry, though only as phases in the development of one tradition. He distinguishes between them as follows:

> The picturesque artists saw the wider range of experience that could be managed by discontinuity and planned irregularity, but they kept to the picture-like single perspective. The interior landscape, however, moves naturally towards the principle of multiple perspectives as in the first two lines of *The Waste Land* where the Christian Chaucer, Sir James Frazer and Jessie Weston are simultaneously present. This is "cubist perspective" which renders, at once, a diversity of views with the spectator always in the centre of the picture, whereas in picturesque art the spectator is always outside. The cubist perspective of interior landscape typically permits an immediacy, a variety and solidity of experience denied to the picturesque and to Tennyson.[1]

Now this, too, immediately recalls Yeats, speaking of Joyce, of Pound, and of Proust:

> This new art which has arisen in different countries simultaneously seems related ... to that form of the new realist philosophy which thinks that the secondary and primary qualities alike are independent of consciousness; that an object can at the same moment have contradictory qualities. This philosophy seems about to follow the analogy of an art that has more rapidly completed itself, and after deciding that a penny is bright and dark, oblong and round, hot and cold, dumb and ringing in its own right; to think of the calculations it incites, our distaste and pleasure at its sight, the decision that made us pitch it, our preference for head or tail, as independent of a consciousness that has shrunk back, grown intermittent and accidental, into the looking-glass ...
>
> If you ask me why I do not accept a doctrine so respectable and convenient, its cruder forms so obviously resurrected to get science down from Berkeley's roasting-spit, I can but answer

[1] McLuhan, *loc. cit.*, pp. 281, 282.

like Zarathustra, "Am I a barrel of memories that I should give you my reasons?"; somewhere among those memories something compels me to reject whatever—to borrow a metaphor of Coleridge's—drives mind into the quicksilver.[1]

There is an obvious relation between McLuhan's cubist perspective offering "at once, a diversity of views", and the new realist philosophy indicated by Yeats, according to which "an object can at the same moment have contradictory qualities". Where McLuhan speaks of "the spectator always in the centre of the picture", Yeats talks, here and elsewhere, of a consciousness withdrawn into the quicksilver at the back of the mirror. The critic and the poet are speaking of the same thing, and in very similar imagery, though from different points of view.

Yeats's appeal to Coleridge is just:

In disciplining the mind one of the first rules should be, to lose no opportunity of tracing words to their origin; one good consequence of which will be, that he will be able to use the *language* of sight without being enslaved by its affections. He will at least save himself from the delusive notion, that what is not *imageable* is likewise not *conceivable*. To emancipate the mind from the despotism of the eye is the first step towards its emancipation from the influences and intrusions of the senses, sensations and passions generally. Thus most effectively is the power of abstraction to be called forth....[2]

This is the Coleridge who admonished Wordsworth that the best part of human language comes from the allocation of fixed symbols to internal acts of the mind. All this side of Coleridge's thought flies in the face of modern poetic theory, symbolist or imagist. And from his point of view, such modern theory is grounded upon the delusion that what cannot be imaged cannot be conceived. According to Coleridge, conceptual thinking outstrips thinking in images; for H. M. McLuhan, as for

[1] Yeats, Introduction to Hone and Rossi: *Bishop Berkeley: His Life, Writings and Philosophy*, pp. xxiv, xxv.
[2] Quoted by Herbert Read, *The True Voice of Feeling*, p. 179.

most symbolist and post-symbolist theorists, the truth is just the other way round—images, if cunningly arranged, can get beyond concepts. At this point, the alignment of forces, for and against authentic syntax in poetry, is particularly clear.

§ 2

Let us try, for the last time, to focus the point at issue, in particular examples. To be fair, we need to compare two whole poems. Here is Pound's "The Gypsy":

> That was the top of the walk, when he said:
> "Have you seen any others, any of our lot,
> With apes or bears?"
>   —a brown upstanding fellow
> Not like the half-castes,
>   up on the wet road near Clermont.
> The wind came, and the rain,
> And mist clotted about the trees in the valley,
> And I'd the long ways behind me,
>   gray Arles and Biaucaire,
> And he said, "Have you seen any of our lot?"
> I'd seen a lot of his lot . . .
>   ever since Rhodez,
> Coming down from the fair
>   of St. John,
> With caravans, but never an ape or a bear.

A similar experience lies behind Wordsworth's "Stepping Westward":

> *What, you are stepping westward?"—"Yea.*"
> —'Twould be a *wildish* destiny,
> If we, who thus together roam
> In a strange land, and far from home,
> Were in this place the guests of Chance:
> Yet who would stop, or fear to advance,
> Though home or shelter he had none,
> With such a sky to lead him on?

The dewy ground was dark and cold;
Behind, all gloomy to behold;
And stepping westward seemed to be
A kind of *heavenly* destiny:
I liked the greeting; 'twas a sound
Of something without place or bound;
And seemed to give me spiritual right
To travel through that region bright.

The voice was soft, and she who spake
Was walking by her native lake:
The salutation had to me
The very sound of courtesy:
Its power was felt; and while my eye
Was fixed upon the glowing sky,
The echo of the voice enwrought
A human sweetness with the thought
Of travelling through the world that lay
Before me in my endless way.

Wordsworth's poem is one I am very fond of; yet it is difficult
to deny that Pound's is much superior. On the other hand, I do
not think its superiority can be defined in terms of concretion
over against abstraction, objective correlative against subjective disquisition.

It is apparent in the first place that Pound's apparently
"free" versification is incomparably stricter than Wordsworth's apparent regularity. Consider only "spiritual right",
and the choking elision to be given to the last three syllables
of "spiritual". Wordsworth's italics, on "wildish" and
"heavenly", ask the reader for an emphasis that Pound would
have forced upon him by an arrangement of rhythms; and they
testify, also, I think to Wordsworth's embarrassment, his sense
of insecurity, about the colloquialisms he employs. Then, too,
Pound is so much more concise. The poems are really strikingly
similar. The impression of illimitable horizons, of "something
without place or bound" (Wordsworth lends himself to quota-
tion, Pound does not—that is part of the difference), receives,

in both poems, a slanting ray of other feeling, towards the end. Wordsworth's "human sweetness" means a recognition that the ardent wanderlust is provided for and sanctioned by popular feeling—the folk know that sort of yearning and acknowledge it as human. Pound's last cadence, "but never an ape or a bear", throws an oblique ray in just the same way, mingling with the predominant emotion a feeling, this time, of wistfulness, even frustration. A very similar arc of feeling is followed in both poems, but by Pound with a far finer economy. And undoubtedly Pound's is a musical syntax, where Wordsworth's is not. For consider: who is "up on the wet road near Clermont"? The authentic Romanies? Or the half-castes with whom they must not be confused? Or the poet himself, and the man he has encountered? We do not know, and it does not matter. For all that is required at this moment in the poem is the "up" and the "on", the release, like the call of a horn, into distance and altitude. Or when was it that "the wind came, and the rain"? Was it when he saw the half-castes, or when he saw the full-blooded gypsies, or in between his meeting either of these and his meeting with the man who addressed him, or finally, did the squall come while he and the man were talking? And again, it doesn't matter. This is a rattle on the percussion as the other was a call of the horn; syntax has become music.

But, if Pound's poem is better than Wordsworth's, it is not better because it is more "concrete" or because its syntax has become music. If it is more concise, it is not for these reasons. On the contrary, what pads out Wordsworth's poem and makes it blowsy is just that part of it where he tries to be specific and to provide "images":

> The dewy ground was dark and cold;
> Behind, all gloomy to behold; ...

But in any case, this is not the point. Is "Stepping Westward" poetry at all? According to McLuhan it cannot be. For its language is most distinguished and affecting just where it is most abstract and conceptual:

> The echo of the voice enwrought
> A human sweetness with the thought
> Of travelling through the world that lay
> Before me in my endless way.

A new quality ("human sweetness") enters into the poet's thinking. Nothing could be much more "abstract" than that. But when all is said and done, Wordsworth's poem is more original than Pound's. That there is a wistfulness at the heart of the wanderlust is no new idea; and that need not matter when the old idea is expressed so memorably as it is by Pound. But Wordsworth's recognition that the wanderlust is acknowledged by traditional sentiment, and that that acknowledgment makes it all the more attractive—that is the sort of idea that could have occurred only to Wordsworth; it is something far more strange and novel.

"Stepping Westward" offends against other canons of modern criticism. It tells us about an experience, instead of presenting it; what happened is described, not embodied. The question whether this is legitimate in poetry is one that has been much debated. And it might seem that the question of poetic syntax is bound up with this; that in order to find room for authentic syntax in poetry, we have to admit that poetry may talk about, describe, comment explicitly on the experiences it presents. As a matter of fact I *would* admit that. But it is important to realize that there is no need to do so, that the issue here debated is *not* the same as that between "talking about" and "presenting". On the contrary, a case for syntax other than symbolist syntax in poetry can be made to rest upon just these grounds—that a movement of syntax can render, immediately present, the curve of destiny through a life or the path of an energy through the mind. It is true that the emphasis on presentation rather than description has tended to exclude authentic syntax from poetry. But that is another matter; in my view the enthusiasts for presentation, for embodiment, have been ill-advised in ignoring the part that authentic syntax can play in bringing about all that they hope for, by miming a movement of the mind or of fate.

There is a muddle in the offing here, about the word "discursive". Mrs. Langer uses it precisely. when she discriminates between discursive and presentational symbolism; by "discursive" she means what moves from point to point. Literary critics frequently use it loosely, to mean an apparently casual musing or meditation, something not far short of "rambling". In Mrs. Langer's sense of the word, the verse of *The Prelude* is discursive; for a poetry depending so much on nicely distinguished verbs must move through them, from point to point in time. It is often called "discursive" in the looser sense also; but my disagreement with Dr. Leavis turned on just that point —in the first version, at any rate, the verse of *The Prelude* does not describe or discuss an experience, it renders it in mime.

This cannot be said of the syntax in "Stepping Westward", a poem which is discursive, I think, in the looser sense. There the comparison with "The Gypsy" was in terms of conciseness. And the point to be made is that Wordsworth comes nearest to the conciseness of Pound at just the point where his language is most conceptual and his syntax correspondingly most rapid.

When all is said and done, there is no way of deciding which is the better poem—"Stepping Westward" or "The Gypsy". In the end we have to admit, there is no comparison. Certainly there is a sense in which one can say Pound's poem is much better *as a poem*. But then it is a queer understanding of "poem" which obliges us, when we judge it as such, to leave out of account all the originality and profundity in what the poem says. This is however what we are forced to do, if we believe with Mrs. Langer that "it is not a proposition, but the entertainment of one" which we should attend to. On this showing, the quality of what is entertained cannot enter into our judgment of the poem as poem. And however handy this may be when we deal with a poet like Yeats, who seems to entertain some very queer customers indeed, it blinds us to the greatness of a poet like Wordsworth, which often resides just in his capacity for making novel discoveries about human sentiment. His entertainment may be shabby, but the company is of the best; yet this, it seems, is just what we have to leave out of account.

It was De Quincey who made much of Wordworth's faculty for sheer "discovery":

A volume might be filled with such glimpses of novelty as Wordsworth has first laid bare, even to the apprehension of the *senses*. For the *understanding*, when moving in the same track of human sensibilities, he has done only not so much. How often must the human heart have felt the case, when there are sorrows which descend far below the region in which tears gather; and yet who has ever given utterance to this feeling until Wordsworth came with his immortal line:

"Thoughts that do often lie too deep for tears"?

This sentiment, and others that might be adduced (such as "The child is father of the man"), have even passed into the popular heart, and are often quoted by those who know not *whom* they are quoting.[1]

This is trite and homely stuff beside the refinements of symbolist aesthetics, but it brings us back to a point made earlier about a line of Shakespeare:

Uneasy lies the head that wears a crown.

This is another line that has "passed into the popular heart", and the point made then was that the pursuit of concretions would banish such a line (for visualize the image, or, more properly, make an image of it, and it is ludicrous). Now, coming upon a similar instance from a quite different direction, we find such a line debarred from poetry once again. Just those lines that have gone over into folk-wisdom are stigmatized as unpoetical. The folk of course can pervert a poetic statement by

[1] *De Quincey's Literary Criticism*, ed. Darbishire, p. 240.

tearing it from its context; there is the notorious case, "One touch of nature makes the whole world kin." Yet this is the exception, not the rule. And there must surely be something wrong with theories that banish from poetry all that part of it which is taken up into popular wisdom. Mrs. Langer is forced to do this, because the folk, when they seize upon a line of poetry, make what is for her the cardinal error of supposing that the poet means just what he says, that the poetic statement he makes is not wholly different from the statements they make themselves, and that the syntax of his statement is not wholly different in function from the syntax they are used to elsewhere.

XIV

THE REEK OF THE HUMAN

✥✥✥✥✥✥✥✥✥✥✥✥✥✥✥✥✥✥✥✥✥✥✥✥✥✥✥

IT will be apparent that the impulse behind all this writing is conservative. But it is, I hope, a rational conservatism. When a poem abjures even the forms of syntax, or when it retains those forms but perverts their function to make syntax into music, or when it uses syntax only incidentally, articulating rather through images spaced by rhythms—when any of these things happen in a poem, I do not say, "This is not poetry at all", or, "This is not poetry as I understand it." I have risked such a sweeping judgment only once, on the sort of poetry represented by the sonnets of Dylan Thomas. I am concerned only to make room in our understanding of what poetry is, for all of the varieties of poetic syntax which I have tried to distinguish. And it is my contention that there is not room for all of them in any one of the theories of poetry which I have considered.

If I am most anxious to show the inadequacy of the symbolist and post-symbolist tradition, it is because that is still the prevailing tradition in criticism and poetic theory (though not any longer, I think, in English poetic practice). By comparison, Fenollosa, though he certainly pushes his insights too far, is thoroughly conservative in spirit, and provides indeed the best antidote to the symbolist excesses.

The tendency of all symbolist theories is to make the world of poetry more autonomous. Most of them, like Mrs. Langer's, stop short of making the world of poetry wholly self-sufficient, and keep open some avenue, however narrow and winding, by which the world of poetry can communicate with the outside world, through mimesis. But some theorists—those, perhaps, who see poetic syntax as mathematics rather than music —seem prepared to cut poetry loose altogether. And here I will use Mr. Northrop Frye, once again, as whipping-boy:

> The assumption in the word "universe", whether applied to physics or to literature, is not that these subjects are descriptive of total existence, but simply that they are in themselves totally intelligible. No one can know the whole of physics at once, but physics would not be a coherent subject unless this were theoretically possible. The argument of Aristotle's *Physics*, which treats physics as the study of motion in nature, leads inexorably to the conception of an unmoved mover at the circumference of the world. In itself this is merely the postulate that the total form of physics is the physical universe. If Christian theology takes physics to be descriptive of an ultra-physical reality or activity, and proceeds to identify this unmoved first mover with an existent God, that is the business of Christian theology: physics as physics will be unaffected by it. The assumption of a verbal universe similarly leads to the conception of an unspeakable first word at its circumference. This in itself is merely the postulate that literature is totally intelligible. If Christian theology identifies this first word with the Word of God or person of Christ, and says that the vision of total human creative power is divine as well as human, the literary critic, as such, is not concerned either to support or to refute the identification.[1]

I go so far as I can in understanding this passage by setting it beside Elizabeth Sewell's very suggestive notion of systems in the mind, some "open" and some "closed", an idea which comes by analogy from mechanics.

Miss Sewell observes that "The mind has a choice of systems within which it can work." She quotes, "The primary control

[1] Frye "Levels of Meaning in Literature," *Kenyon Review*, xii, 2, pp. 260, 261

of the concepts of mathematics is that contradiction should not be involved." And she goes on:

> Nightmare works in reverse, including all that is disorder and excluding all that is order. In the one system there is the certainty of the expected, in the other the certainty of the unexpected, but in neither system is there any room for probability or uncertainty.[1]

It should now be plain that Mr. Frye's rhetoric converts language from an open system into a closed one. In literature, on his view, there is the certainty of the intelligible, and there is therefore no room in it for probability or uncertainty. Literature is certain to find what it seeks because its conclusions are implicit in its postulate. But then, our mistake is in thinking that it seeks anything. It does not seek, it constructs:

> The poet's new poem merely articulates what was already latent in the order of words, and the assumption of a single order of words is as fundamental to the poet as the assumption of a single order of nature is to the natural scientist. The difficulty in understanding this arises from the confusion of language with dictionary language, and of literature with the bibliography of literature. Language in a human mind is not a list of words with their customary meanings attached, but a single interlocking structure, one's total power of expressing oneself. Literature is the objective counterpart of this, a total form of verbal expression which is re-created in miniature whenever a new poem is written.[2]

This emphasis on "articulation", on "a single interlocking structure", rather than on "words with their customary meanings attached", seems to promise well for poetic syntax. But a moment's thought will reveal that these expressions make a case for syntax on still other grounds than the several we have discussed already. For if the words in poetry are to be considered in their relations with each other, not in their relations

[1] Elizabeth Sewell, *The Structure of Poetry*, p. 64.
[2] Frye, *loc. cit.*, p. 260.

to "their customary meanings", syntax in the same way is to be considered, not in its relation to anything outside the realm of language, but in relation to "a total form of verbal expression". This syntax articulates, not "the world", but "the world of the poem".

It is quite natural, therefore, for Mr. Frye to pronounce:

> The relation of literature to factual verbal structures has to be established from within one of the latter. Literature must be approached centrifugally, from the outside, if we are to get any factual significance out of it.... One begins talking about "Lycidas", for instance, by itemizing all the things that "Lycidas" illustrates in the non-literary verbal world: English history in 1637, the Church and Milton's view of it, the position of Milton as a young poet planning an epic and a political career, the literary convention of the pastoral elegy, Christian teachings on the subject of death and resurrection, and so on. It would be quite possible to spend a whole critical life in this allegorical limbo of background, without ever getting to the poem at all, or even feeling the need of doing so.[1]

"Lycidas" is an apt example, of course. But take Wordsworth's "Complaint of a Forsaken Indian Woman". The whole point of this poem lies in its truth to human nature; and is it really true that, to get its factual significance, as presenting the feelings of a woman separated from her child, we need to come at it from within a "factual verbal structure", that is, presumably, through a treatise on the psychology of mother and child? We need, it is true, to have some humanity ourselves; but is that searching of our own hearts an "allegorical limbo of background"? And when we come out of that limbo and get to the poem, what is left for us to get to? Once we have taken the truth of the poem to a human predicament, there is nothing left; for diction, metre, rhyme, imagery, all are made transparent for the truth to shine out through them. This poem is not a world, like the world of a symbolist poem, "closed and self-sufficient, being the pure system of the ornaments and the

[1] Frye, *loc. cit.* p. 250.

chances of language." It takes on meaning only as it is open to another world; unless it refers to that other "real" world, it is meaningless. Its syntax articulates not just itself, not only its own world, but the world of common experience.

The appeal of theories such as Mr. Frye's is manifest in the loaded words that their promoters use, in recommending them. A poetry in which the syntax articulates only "the world of the poem" is said to be "pure", "absolute", "sheer", "self-sufficient". Wordsworth's poems are "impure" because they have about them the smell of soil and soiled flesh, the reek of humanity. Their syntax is not "pure" syntax because it refers to, it mimes, something outside itself and outside the world of its poem, something that smells of the human, of generation and hence of corruption. It is my case against the symbolist theorists that, in trying to remove the human smell from poetry, they are only doing harm. For poetry to be great, it must reek of the human, as Wordsworth's poetry does. This is not a novel contention; but perhaps it is one of those things that cannot be said too often.

APPENDIX

HULME, MRS. LANGER, AND FENOLLOSA ON THE RELATION OF POETRY TO SCIENCE

I T is instructive to compare my three main authorities—Hulme, Fenollosa, and Mrs. Langer—from the point of view of the attitudes they adopt to scientific thought.

Hulme takes scientific explanation as the type of "the extensive manifold". According to him, because the scientist is committed to explanation of this sort, he is satisfied only when he finds it, and the phenomena which are of the other, intensive sort are not acknowledged, merely because they do not suit the mental machinery. Hulme takes, "as an example of the kind of thing the intellect does consider perfectly clear and comprehensible", the image of pieces on a draughtboard:

> You find as a matter of fact that any science, as it tends towards perfection, tends to present reality as consisting of something exactly similar to this draughtboard. They all resolve the complex phenomena of nature into fixed separate elements changing only in position. They all adopt atomic theories, and the model of all the sciences is astronomy. In order to get a convenient nomenclature one calls all complex things which can be resolved into separate elements or atoms in this way "extensive manifolds".[1]

But later, when he discusses the Bergsonian concepts of time and change, he changes his image for the scientific outlook, from draughts to billiards:

> One can get a picture of the type in terms of which the mind insists on conceiving change by thinking of the motion of

[1] Hulme, *Speculations*, pp. 176, 177.

billiard balls on an ideally smooth table where there is no friction. It would be impossible here to discover or conceive the existence of freedom. There is in fact no change at all. You can predict with certainty the position of the balls at any future moment, for you have a fixed number of elements moving under fixed laws.

But—and here comes one of the most important elements for the understanding of what Bergson is getting at—this is only a true account of change if you admit that everything can in reality be analysed into separate elements like the balls on the table. If it can, then the future must be determined; but we have just seen that mental life at the level of the fundamental self cannot. It is an interpenetrating whole: it is not composed of elements. It changes, but the way in which it changes will not fit into the kind of conception which the intellect forms of change.[1]

This conception of the scientific outlook was already outdated in Hulme's time, but its obsolescence was only later brought home to the general reader, by Eddington:

The recognition that our knowledge of the objects treated in physics consists solely of readings of pointers and other indicators transforms our view of the status of physical knowledge in a fundamental way. Until recently it was taken for granted that we had knowledge of a far more intimate kind of the entities of the external world. ... The Victorian physicist felt that he knew just what he was talking about when he used such terms as *matter* and *atoms*. Atoms were tiny billiard balls, a crisp statement that was supposed to tell you all about their nature in a way which could never be achieved for transcendental things like consciousness, beauty, and humour.[2]

It will hardly be supposed the Eddington's world will recommend itself to Hulme any more than the world of the Victorian physicist. A pointer-reading is even more "abstract" than an atom. On the other hand, to a theorist for whom words are verbal symbols, Eddington's science recommends itself at once.

[1] Hulme, *op. cit.*, p. 192.
[2] Eddington, *The Nature of the Physical World*, pp. 258, 259.

For Hulme Eddington only widens the gap between poetry and science; but for Susanne Langer he has closed it, for the pointer-readings of the physicist are seen to be a language of symbols interposed between him and experience, just as a language of non-verbal symbols is interposed for the mathematician and the musician.

As for Fenollosa, his attitude to science emerges from his attitude to the traditional grammarians and their backers, the logicians:

> Of course this view of the grammarians springs from the discredited, or rather the useless, logic of the Middle Ages. According to this logic, thought deals with abstractions, concepts drawn out of things by a sifting process. These logicians never inquired how the "qualities" which they pulled out of things came to be there. The truth of all their little checker-board juggling depended upon the natural order by which these powers or properties or qualities were folded in concrete things, yet they despised the "thing" as a mere "particular", or pawn. It was as if Botany should reason from the leaf-patterns woven into our tablecloths. Valid scientific thought consists in following as closely as may be the actual and entangled lines of forces as they pulse through things. Thought deals with no bloodless concepts but science watches *things move* under its microscope.[1]

This seems quite close in places to Hulme's Bergsonian distinction between intensive and extensive manifolds; the qualities, powers, and principles that for Fenollosa are "folded in concrete things", are the things that for Hulme and Pound are "unfolded" in the extensive manifold of syntax, though Hulme thinks that some of them resist that process. But there is the significant difference that according to Fenollosa the scientist stands for "the thing", along with the poet, over against the logician.

[1] Physics is not the only science. Fenollosa here appeals to botany. And it is notable that when Pound restates Fenollosa's position for him, he finds his example in biology, a science still far from pointer-readings and mathematics.

This is no doubt a necessary correction of Hulme's emphasis. The continually renewed hostility between the experimental scientist and the rationalist is a fact of history for which Hulme, and others like him who put a gulf between science and poetry, make no provision. But Fenollosa does not stop here. Hating abstraction as fiercely as Hulme, he flies in Hulme's face to assert that, wherever else abstraction is found, it is not found in the literature of science. Having castigated, through a couple of harsh and brilliant pages, the methods of mediaeval logic, he blames this habit of mind, as Hulme had blamed the "extensive manifold" habit, for the difficulty that was found in accommodating the idea of evolution:

> It is impossible to represent change in this system or any kind of growth.
> This is probably why the conception of evolution came so late to Europe. It could not make way *until it was prepared to destroy inveterate logic of classification.*

So, for Fenollosa, the acceptance of the idea of evolution represents a triumph for the scientist over the logician:

> Science fought till she got at the things.

And a few lines later:

> In diction and in grammatical form science is utterly opposed to logic. Primitive men who created language agreed with science and not with logic.
> Poetry agrees with science and not with logic.

Plainly, this position is miles away from Hulme's.

It may now be clear how Fenollosa's Augustan air is so revealing. Though he is as averse as Hulme to endorsing the "billiard-balls" of the Victorian physicist, he is even further than Hulme from endorsing Einstein's and Eddington's world of "pointer-readings". His view of science, and his affection for it, go back to the very dawn of modern natural philosophy, further than Newton, back to the world of Robert Boyle and the Royal Society, a world of "things" that act upon one another, the heyday of experimental optimism. Boyle and his fellows were fierce anti-Rationalists, who set up Bacon in opposition to Descartes. That distinction fell to the ground with Newton:

> It is true that Newton, a tireless experimenter and a distruster of theories, astonished his age, but his principal work represented a triumph for Descartes and the mechanical philosophy more than for experimental science.[1]

And the billiard-balls of the Victorian physicist were in sight as soon as Locke distinguished between primary and secondary qualities, and posited the abstract "substance", matter. This point is worth making because it explains, I think, why Fenollosa's views of poetic language and syntax are particularly helpful to the reader of the poetry of just Boyle's period; and also because it helps to explain the relevance, at a later stage of this discussion, of Berkeley, Locke's most powerful critic.

[1] R. F. Jones, "The Background of the Attack on Science in the Age of Pope", in *Pope and his Contemporaries: Essays presented to George Sherburn*, p. 111.

INDEX

Allt, Peter, 129
Alves, Robert, 57
Aristotle, 8, 38, 41, 42, 162

Bacon, Francis, 1, 4, 79, 170
Barbauld, Mrs., 60
Barfield, Owen, 142, 143, 144
Barnes, George, 125
Bell, Clive, 15
Bergson, Henri, 6–9, 13, 22, 47, 133n, 166, 167
Berkeley, George, 117–124, 140, 152, 170
Blake, William, 80–85
Boyle, Robert, 169, 170
Brett, R. L., 106n
Brower, R. A., 54
Brown, Dr. John, 59
Browning, Robert, 74, 79
Burke, Kenneth, 86, 87
Byron, George Gordon, Lord, 30, 56, 57, 60, 61, 62, 63, 79, 95

Carroll, Lewis, 11–12
Cassirer, Ernst, 22
Catullus, 149, 151
Chaucer, Geoffrey, 52, 152
Chapman, George, 4
Coleridge, S. T., 7, 61, 69, 70, 72, 73, 74, 75, 76, 81, 85, 107, 108, 109, 112, 122, 126, 153
Coombes, H, 83
Cowper, William, 52, 80
Crabbe, George, 61, 62

Daniel, Samuel, 46, 47, 48, 50
Dante, 151
Davies, Hugh Sykes, 145
De La Mare, Walter, 147
Denham, Sir John, 56, 57, 59, 61, 62, 94, 95
De Quincey, Thomas, 75, 159
Descartes, René, 117, 170
Donne, John, 53, 54, 134–135
Dryden, John, 60, 61, 79, 98, 99

Eddington, Sir Arthur, 167, 168, 169
Edgeworth, Maria, 60
Edgeworth, Richard Lovell, 60, 62
Eliot, T. S., 21, 30–31, 67, 86, 88–89, 90–91, 125, 129, 140, 141, 148, 150, 152
Ellmann, Richard, 124, 151
Elton, Sir Oliver, 61
Empson, William, 111, 112

Fenollosa, Ernest, 33–55, 56, 66, 67, 80, 95, 96, 97, 99, 100, 101, 107, 108, 116, 118, 119, 120, 122, 123, 125, 131, 132, 133, 134, 136, 144, 161, 166, 168, 169, 170
Flaubert, Gustave, 100, 101
Frye, Northrop, 130–136, 137, 139, 141, 162–165

Gide, André, 97, 100
Gogol, Nikolai, 73, 74
Graves, Robert, 68
Grierson, Sir H. J. C., 95

171

Gris, Juan, 31
Gumilev, Nikolai, 39n

Hackett, C. A., 127
Hartley, David, 112, 115
Herbert, George, 54
Hofmannsthal, Hugo von, 1–5, 9, 99, 100, 105, 110, 151
Hopkins, G. M., 19, 89, 90, 150n
Hough, Graham, 59
Hughes, Jabez, 57
Hulme, T. E., 5–13, 22, 23, 38, 39, 54, 56, 61, 65, 66, 96, 97, 98, 100, 102, 119, 121, 122, 123, 142, 166, 167, 168, 169
Hume, David, 118

Jeffrey, Francis, 56, 57, 60, 61, 62
Jespersen, 70, 108, 142, 144
Johnson, Samuel, 60, 61
Jones, John, 115–116
Jones, R. F., 170
Jonson, Ben, 131–132
Joyce, James, 19, 124, 135, 144, 152

Kahnweiler, D. H., 31
Keats, John, 84–85, 100, 104, 147
Kenner, Hugh, 20, 33, 40–42, 79, 98, 100–101, 117, 118
Kipling, Rudyard, 79

Laforgue, Jules, 149, 151
Landor, Walter Savage, 62, 122–123, 125
Langer, Susanne K., 14–23, 24, 26, 28, 30, 38, 56, 66, 85, 86, 88, 129, 151, 158, 160, 161, 166, 168
Lawrence, D. H., 90
Lear, Edward, 12
Leavis, F. R., 76, 102, 110–115, 122, 158
Lewis, C. Day, 140
Lewis, C. S., 102

Lewis, Percy Wyndham, 133n
Locke, John, 38, 117, 118, 170

McLuhan, H. M., 33, 79, 80, 138, 149, 150, 151, 152, 153, 156
Madan, Julia, 57, 59
Mallarmé, Stephane, 91, 92, 94, 148, 149
Milbourn, 58, 59
Mill, John Stuart, 65
Milton, John, 21, 54, 62, 102, 103, 110, 148, 164
Murphy, Richard, 143, 144, 146

Nabokov, Vladimir, 73, 74
Nemerov, Howard, 10
Newbery, John, 58
Newton, Sir Isaac, 97, 106, 169, 170
Nietzsche, 6

Ozell, 58

Pater, Walter, 15
Paulhan, Jean, 137, 138; 139, 140
Perse, St.-J., 90, 97, 100, 101, 102, 106, 107, 109, 110, 121, 139, 151
Pollock, T. C., 10, 13, 103, 108
Pope, Alexander, 30, 33, 56, 57, 58, 59, 60, 61, 62, 63, 64, 79, 80, 81, 82, 84, 94, 95, 115, 138, 139
Pound, Ezra, 8, 19, 20, 33, 34, 35, 37, 40, 67, 97, 100, 101, 104, 105, 110, 119, 124, 125, 128, 129, 134, 152, 154–158, 168
Prince, F. T., 32, 92–93
Proust, Marcel, 101, 152

Ransom, John Crowe, 6
Read, Sir Herbert, 6, 14, 15, 30, 61, 75, 90, 153n
Richards, I. A., 15, 21, 65, 69
Rilke, Rainer Maria, 9, 19
Rimbaud, Arthur, 126, 129, 138

Rochester, John Wilmot, Earl of, 70
Rodgers, W. R., 13, 19
Roethke, Theodore, 86, 87
Rogers, Samuel, 56, 57
Roscommon, Wentworth Dillon, Earl of, 58, 59, 99
Ruchon, François, 127

Sackville, Thomas, 24–32, 33, 52, 59, 79, 80
Schiller, 31
Scott, Sir Walter, 56
Sewell, Elizabeth, 11–12, 20, 91n, 126, 127, 129, 162–163
Shakespeare, William, 49–52, 54, 55, 76–79, 80, 116, 146, 148, 159
Shelley, Percy Bysshe, 33, 100
Sidney, Sir Philip, 33, 43–46, 48, 50, 52, 53, 54, 130, 139
Sitwell, Edith, 19
Slonim, Marc, 39n
Smart, Christopher, 135, 139
Spenser, Edmund, 47, 54
Spurgeon, C. F. E., 57n
Swart, J., 27
Swift, Jonathan, 80, 82, 94

Tate, Allen, 90, 146
Tennyson, Alfred, Lord, 148, 150

"Thersites", 145
Thierry-Maulnier, 31
Thomas, Dylan, 10, 125–127, 128, 161
Thomas, Edward, 140, 141
Tiller, Terence, 9, 11
Tuve, Rosemund, 22, 25, 52, 53, 54, 124

Valéry, Paul, 12, 20, 21, 91, 94, 104, 105, 107, 109, 110, 121, 139, 149
Vaughan, Henry, 48
Verlaine, Paul, 150
Vico, G., 19

Waller, Edmund, 56, 57, 62
Whitman, Walt, 90
Williams, William Carlos, 19
Wilson, Edmund, 149, 150, 151
Wimsatt, W. K., 139
Winters, Yvor, 150n
Woolf, Virginia, 15–16
Wordsworth, William, 29, 33, 38, 61, 71, 72, 74, 75, 76, 95, 106–116, 118, 122, 144, 149, 150, 153, 154–160, 164, 165

Yeats, W. B., 95, 123–125, 129, 141, 151, 152, 153, 158